icons of jazz

icons of
Jazz

Dave Gelly

THUNDER BAY
P·R·E·S·S

Published in 2000 by
Thunder Bay Press
An imprint of the Advantage Publishers Group
5880 Oberlin Drive, San Diego, CA 92121-4794
www.advantagebooksonline.com

North American edition
Publisher: Ann Ghublikian
Managing Editor: JoAnn Padgett
Project Editor: Elizabeth McNulty

ISBN 1-57145-268-0
Library of Congress Cataloging-in-Publication Data available upon request.

Produced by **Brown Partworks Ltd**
8 Chapel Place, Rivington Street, London EC2A 3DQ, UK
www.brownpartworks.co.uk
Managing Editor: Lindsey Lowe
Project Editor: Dawn Titmus
Design: Bradley Davis

Picture Credits
Archive Photos: Metronome 139, Bob Parent 108, 120, 142, 156; **Arena Images:** Jak Kilby
88; **Corbis:** 132, Jim Boug 167, Frank Driggs/Corbis-Bettmann 132, Roger Ressmeyer 76;
Hulton-Getty: 11, 102, 106, 168, 170; **Robert Hunt Library:** 62; **Herman Leonard:** 8, 14,
26, 44, 48, 57, 64, 66, 82, 100, 104, 114, 126, 128, 136, 138, 148, 159, 166; **Pictorial Press
Limited:** 56; **Pictorial Press/Showtime:** 124; **Popperfoto:** 70, 122; **Redferns:** Mike
Cameron 112, Fin Costello 60, William Gottlieb 16, 40, 50, 68, 78, 84, 90, 92, 94, 110, 144,
Max Jones Files 18, 134, Michael Ochs Archive 10, 20, 32, 80, 86, 96, 152, 154, 162,176,
Andrew Putler 118, 160, David Redfern 22, 24, 30, 42, 52, 54, 58, 72, 98, 116, 140, 151, 164,
172, Chuck Stewart 34, 36, 38, 46, Bob Willoughby 12, 28; **Rex Features:** 146.

Front and back cover: Miles Davis, **Hulton-Getty**
Title page: Roland Kirk, **Hulton-Getty**

Printed and bound in Hong Kong
1 2 3 4 5 00 01 02 03 04

Contents

Introduction

A hundred years ago, jazz was an obscure form of street music flourishing in New Orleans, a seaport on the Gulf of Mexico. It was not unique. Most cities, especially ports, had their own music at the time, but it was jazz—not the tango, habanera, fado, or flamenco—that grew and evolved to become the basis of the entire world's popular music. How did this come about?

Jazz was lucky in the time and place of its birth. It was born with the new century, in a nation destined to become the greatest economic and industrial power in the world. Also born at around the same time were radio and the techniques of sound recording. Put these all together and it is clear that jazz had a huge evolutionary advantage over other forms of urban music. This enabled it to become the first form of popular music to travel beyond its home territory.

In the past, all music was live. If people wanted to hear it, they had to go to where it was being played. The only way of preserving music, so that the same thing could be heard at different times and by more than one audience, was by writing it down. That was how the European classical tradition became established. A composer wrote the music and players trained in standard skills performed it. But most of the world's music is not composer's music; it is and always has been performer's music.

Before Thomas Edison discovered a way to record sound, and Emile Berliner invented the mass-produced gramophone disc, many rich musical cultures must have risen and died, leaving no trace. The Original Dixieland Jazz Band's first record (1917) may not be a great work of art, but it marks a profound change in the history of culture. Similarly, the growth of radio through the 1920s meant that people did not even have to be within earshot of a spinning record. Music could be turned on and off, like tap water.

Naturally, once musicians were able to be heard speaking with their own voices, the voices themselves became a vital part of what was said. That is where the whole notion of a "jazz icon" comes in. Over the course of the 20th century, certain artists had a special appeal. People feel that they know them. Either they set new standards or new styles, such as Louis Armstrong and Charlie Parker, or they attracted a following because of what they seemed to stand for, such as Bunk Johnson, or simply they were so unusual that they stood out, such as the remarkable Roland Kirk.

The majority are black Americans, but if jazz ever was a purely ethnic music (and it seems increasingly doubtful), this long ago ceased to be the case. First it became an all-American idiom, and then spread around the world. Its appeal was so strong that even the most brutal repression failed to silence it. In occupied

Paris during World War II, Django Reinhardt, a Gypsy, played on under the noses of the Nazi authorities.

Strictly, of course, an icon is an object of veneration or worship. In some cases, this would not be putting it too strongly. Louis Armstrong, Duke Ellington, Charlie Parker, and John Coltrane could all be described as icons in this sense. Imitation is said to be the sincerest form of flattery, and that accounts for another large group of icons. To take just three tenor saxophonists—Coleman Hawkins, Lester Young, and Michael Brecker—all have been the subjects of countless imitators, from Japan to Iceland.

It has often been noted that jazz has traveled the distance in a single century that it took European music many centuries to accomplish, from folk music to postmodernism. The mass media speeded up the spread of ideas, and therefore the course of history. As time became telescoped in this way, the stylistic generations overlapped. Louis Armstrong and Charlie Parker were less than 20 years apart in age, and Parker and Ornette Coleman only 10 years apart. In European terms, it was like having Bach, Beethoven, and Schoenberg all alive at the same time. Apart from a few early casualties, such as Parker and Jelly Roll Morton, virtually every major name in jazz was alive and working throughout the 1950s.

Critics gave little thought to this remarkable state of affairs, apparently assuming that it would go on for ever. But with the deaths of Armstrong and Ellington, in 1971 and 1974, respectively, a subtle change came over jazz. It was forced to acknowledge the fact that it had a history, a canon of great work by dead artists, that "new" did not necessarily mean "better," and that the music had become so diverse that, among those who called themselves jazz lovers, very few indeed were going to listen to every style of jazz. Just like European classical music, in fact.

So the status of icon is not something officially bestowed, like a medal. But, however one cares to describe them, and however one may differ from individual choices, the 84 figures in this book all inspired admiration and affection among jazz lovers and made an indelible mark on the course of jazz history.

Dave Gelly.

Cannonball Adderley

He was called "Cannonball" not because of his round, portly figure, nor on account of his blindingly fast alto saxophone technique. It was his healthy appetite that led fellow schoolkids in Tampa, Florida, to dub Julian Adderley "Cannibal." Who can blame him for making a slight adjustment to the childhood nickname?

A child prodigy, Adderley was teaching saxophone in Florida schools while still a teenager, and successfully leading his own band. He finally yielded to the urgings of his admirers and moved to New York in 1955, at age 27. By sheer chance, he arrived very soon after the death of Charlie Parker, when the entire jazz world was waiting for the next great alto voice to emerge. Adderley's ripe, blues-filled tone and immensely fluent improvisation made an immediate impact. The fact that his style was heavily influenced by Parker at the time only served to encourage excited claims that here was the "new Bird."

But Cannonball was his own man, and with growing self-confidence, his true originality quickly emerged. At times his playing could be so ornate that listeners were left gasping for breath; at other times he adopted the simple, declamatory style of rhythm and blues. By alternating the two, he could create endless patterns of musical light and shade.

And he was ever open to new ideas and influences. In 1957 he joined Miles Davis's band, turning it from a quintet into a sextet. From Miles he picked up the idea of using space as a significant element in improvisation, and with the band's other saxophonist, John Coltrane, he worked on the concept of playing on modes and scales in place of chords. The whole thing came together in one of the most enduring classics of jazz history, Miles's 1959 album, *Kind of Blue*.

Later that year Adderley formed a quintet with his younger brother, Nat, on cornet. This was the band that finally brought him the acclaim he deserved. The early sixties was a time of growing black consciousness and a new interest in the heritage of black America. The key word in this movement was "soul," and Adderley's "soul jazz," with its blues sonority and gospel cadences, caught the mood of the time exactly. The band had many hits with pieces in this style, including such titles as "Sack o'Woe," "Work Song," and "The Sermonette," composed by Nat, and "Mercy, Mercy, Mercy," the work of the band's Austrian-born pianist, Joe Zawinul.

Cannonball Adderley combined the harmonic sophistication and technical brilliance of bebop with the simple emotionalism of blues and gospel music to create a new genre, soul jazz, perfectly in tune with the times. His albums consistently topped the jazz charts and his quintet drew capacity crowds wherever it appeared.

Louis Armstrong

1 9 0 1 - 1 9 7 1

For most of his life, Louis Armstrong was the much-loved entertainer "Satchmo"—a kind of international teddy bear. He was also a modest, generous, and sweet-natured man. But a person can be all those things without being a genius, and Armstrong was a genius. If he had not been born in New Orleans at the beginning of the 20th century, if he had not been sent to the Home for Colored Waifs at age 11 and learned the cornet there, jazz might not have developed in the way it did—in which case the history of Western music, and therefore of Western culture, would have taken a different course. That is how important Louis Armstrong is.

From the moment he joined King Oliver's band in Chicago in 1922, Armstrong was marked out as special. His playing was not just better than other people's, it was quite different. It reduced what had previously been a set of vague notions about "hot music" to one basic idea—a fluid, improvised line deployed over a regular beat and a repeated harmonic sequence. That has been the recipe for virtually the whole of jazz ever since, and no-one ever did it more elegantly or profoundly or with greater wit, logic, or passion.

Above: A publicity shot of Armstrong and Lucille, Armstrong's fourth wife, taken in Rome in 1949. Lucille provided Armstrong with the first stable home life he had ever known.

Through the 1920s, his trumpet playing and his unique, honey-and-gravel singing voice were endlessly imitated. His recordings, such as "Potato Head Blues" and "Struttin' with Some Barbecue," supplied the model that taught the rest of the world the grammar, vocabulary, and syntax of jazz. In the 1930s, Armstrong took over leadership of Luis Russell's orchestra, touring as a star soloist and making his debut in movies. There was something irresistible about his very presence—the vast, welcoming smile and conspiratorial chuckle.

From 1947 until his death, Louis led his All-Stars. Some of Armstrong's best work was recorded with the All-Stars, such as the classic albums *Louis Armstrong Plays W.C. Handy* (1954) and *Satchmo—A Musical Autobiography* (1956–57).

Left: Although he started out playing cornet, Louis switched to trumpet in the late 1920s, partly for its more brilliant tone and partly because it looked more glamorous. This publicity shot from the late 1930s captures perfectly his carefree, mischievous persona of those days. This was the Louis who first attracted a mass popular audience.

Chet Baker

1 9 2 9 - 1 9 8 8

Chesney Baker was blessed and cursed in roughly equal measure. His blessings included a natural affinity for the trumpet, a beautiful, delicate tone, and a phenomenally accurate musical ear. As a young man he was also spectacularly good-looking in a James Dean-ish way. The curse he bore was an addictive personality, which laid waste to his career, blighted his relationships, and ruined his health.

The jazz world at large first learned about Chet Baker in 1952, as a member of a highly successful quartet led by baritone sax player Gerry Mulligan. Critics hailed Baker as the "new Miles Davis," and even "the new Bix Beiderbecke," on account of his light sound and tuneful style.

Although Chet was to become the more notorious addict, it was Gerry who got busted and imprisoned first, leaving Chet free to form his own quartet, in 1953, in which he both played and sang. His singing was as soft and light as his trumpet, devoid of the usual vocalist's tricks and more in tune than most full-time singers. He recorded ballad albums with strings and jazz albums with some of the finest players of the day. He could have had it all—"James Dean, Sinatra, and Bix, rolled into one," as one commentator put it. But by the end of the 1950s, his erratic, heroin-induced behavior had transformed him from the Golden Boy into an untouchable.

He was busted in New York and imprisoned, then fled to Europe. There, he made several attempts to resume his career, supported each time by a new, devoted woman, convinced that she was the one who could save him from himself. He was imprisoned again, this time in Italy in 1960, fled to Germany, and was deported back to the U.S. in 1961. In San Francisco, in a fight over a heroin deal, his teeth were smashed beyond repair. Somehow, he kept playing, even when there was no-one to listen. It was bad luck to be around Chet and people naturally avoided him.

In his last years he managed to salvage something from the wreckage. On a methadone program, toothless and looking older than his years, he resumed touring and was hailed, especially in Europe, as a kind of Beat Generation hero. A documentary film, *Let's Get Lost* (1988), was made about his life. He made more records, including a glorious set with the German NDR Big Band, and was looking cautiously to the future when he died after falling from the window of an Amsterdam hotel room.

In his early twenties, Chet Baker had the looks of James Dean and the musical charisma of a latter-day Bix Beiderbecke. He could have been the first jazz megastar, but drug addiction and terms of imprisonment prematurely aged him. Thirty years after this picture was taken, he was wizened and toothless.

Count Basie

1904 - 1984

Bink, bink—bink! Three tiny icicles of sound drop into a brief pool of silence, followed by the final Niagara roar of brass, saxophones, and drums—the classic ending to a number by Count Basie and his Orchestra, and it never fails.

Bill Basie led his band for more than half a century, and only Ellington, in his totally different way, is worthy of comparison. Basie was the master of swing: simple, clear, uncluttered, four-beats-to-the-bar, irresistible swing. He sat at the piano, to one side of the band, with his matchless rhythm section close at hand, directing the proceedings with nods, winks, and the occasional flick of a finger.

Born in Red Bank, New Jersey, Basie served his apprenticeship in traveling shows, finally joining Bennie Moten's band in Kansas City in 1929. When Moten died in 1935, the nucleus of his band stayed together as a nine-piece under Basie's leadership. Discovered by the great jazz talent-spotter John Hammond, and expanded first to 14 and then to 16 members, they came to New York in 1936, a ragged but immensely exciting team, bursting with energy and packed with great soloists—Buck Clayton on trumpet, Lester Young and Herschel Evans on tenor saxophones, and the phenomenal Jo Jones on drums.

Right through the swing era and the years of World War II, Basie and the band toured the dance halls and theaters of the U.S., often in appalling conditions. Unlike other band leaders, many of whom were heartily disliked by their musicians, Basie traveled in the bus with the others, one of the boys, playing poker through the night and swapping stories. Like all traveling bands, Basie's team became a very close-knit social unit, closer than many families. Friendships formed among them during those days often endured for life.

As the years passed, the sound of the band changed. By the 1950s, it had developed into a sleek, swinging machine, and Basie had refined and polished his own playing down to almost nothing. But the tiny sliver that remained was a thing of wonder, a distillation of pure time. It was also a source of despair to all other jazz pianists because it was impossible to copy. Basie did so little, and how do you copy a man not doing something?

By the time of his death, Basie and the band had long achieved the status of an international institution. There is still a Count Basie Orchestra in existence, sounding remarkably like the original, but no-one could ever quite replace the man himself.

Basie was the most undemonstrative of leaders, conducting his band with just a pointing finger and raised eyebrows. He disliked talking about himself and was always full of praise for others, pianists included. He loved to reminisce about the old days, especially his youthful exploits in Kansas City.

Sidney Bechet

1 8 9 7 - 1 9 5 9

Sidney Bechet was the first important jazz saxophonist. He switched from clarinet to soprano saxophone because the latter had a louder, more commanding sound, and Bechet was a man who liked to make his presence felt. His playing reflected his character to perfection—passionate, wilful, domineering, and totally self-assured.

Born in New Orleans of comfortably off French Creole stock, Bechet was a child prodigy who began playing professionally while still a teenager. Almost from the outset he was presented as a virtuoso soloist with big touring musical productions. His travels took him to Britain, France, Germany, and even as far as Russia. In most of these places, Bechet's playing was the first jazz people had ever heard and it came as a revelation. In 1919 the great Swiss conductor Ernest Ansermet hailed him as "an artist of genius."

Because he was away from the U.S. for long periods at a crucial time in jazz development, Bechet did not build himself a career, unlike his New Orleans contemporary, Louis Armstrong. When he returned in the early 1930s, he was devastated to find that his style of jazz was now considered corny and out-of-date. Musical work was hard to come by, and to make ends meet, he opened a tailor's shop in New York. Even so, it was during this lean period that he made some of his finest records, including tracks with his New Orleans Feetwarmers and duet sessions with clarinettist Mezz Mezzrow.

As Bechet entered his fifties, his fortunes picked up. The "revivalist" movement, rediscovering music and musicians of the jazz past, was gathering strength and adopted him as one of its figureheads. He was invited to Paris in 1949 to appear at the city's first Jazz Fair, and there began the final, extraordinary period of Sidney Bechet's remarkable life. The whole of France seemed to fall in love with him and, since he considered himself to be a species of Frenchman in any case, he returned the compliment. He moved to Paris, married an heiress, Elisabeth Ziegler, and had a son, Daniel, by his mistress, Jacqueline Pekaldi.

Throughout the 1950s, Bechet was one of the most popular stars in France. His records sold in millions, rivaling even those of Edith Piaf in popularity. To this day, film and TV directors intent on recreating the atmosphere of that time have only to include a snatch of Bechet on the soundtrack. After his death his statue was erected near his Antibes home, in the square that bears his name.

In the last decade of his life, Bechet's soprano saxophone became part of the soundtrack of French life. "He was a faraway idol, whose music resounded in cafés and glided across the busy boulevard to our rooms in the Cité," wrote Persian poet Sasha Guppy, recalling her student days in Paris.

Bix Beiderbecke

1903 - 1931

Bix Beiderbecke was the first white jazz hero. His story, told and retold, has influenced the way jazz musicians are depicted in popular reportage and fiction ever since. The whole romantic cliché of genius, drink, drugs, self-destruction, and early death begins with him.

Bix was born in Davenport, Iowa, into a well-off and very respectable German–American family. Davenport lies on the Mississippi, and when Bix was a boy, it was the upriver terminus for the great excursion paddle-steamers from New Orleans and the South. Bix would hang around the landing stage, listening to the bands playing on deck. He also acquired some of the first records by the Original Dixieland Jazz Band. He had a phenomenally quick ear and copied the sounds he heard, first on the family piano and later on a borrowed cornet. He was, and remained, entirely self-taught. Despite all efforts to encourage, educate, and bully him into becoming a solid citizen, Bix ended up as a jazz musician—which, in the Prohibition era of the 1920s, meant a disreputable, gin-drinking member of the unreliable classes.

At 20 he played and recorded with the Wolverines, a decent enough little band but not in his class. Later he joined the more prestigious Gene Goldkette Orchestra and, finally, the huge, vastly popular "symphonic jazz" outfit of Paul Whiteman. He was immensely proud of this achievement. Joining Whiteman meant that he could claim to be a success in his chosen field and not, after all, the black sheep of the family. He sent home copies of every record he made with Whiteman. The parcels were never opened.

Bix's best work can be heard on records made by small groups drawn from the Goldkette and Whiteman ranks. His bright, bubbling phrases and a tone that someone once described as "like hitting a bell" make him one of the most instantly attractive soloists in the whole of jazz. There is an optimistic, innocent quality about such pieces as "Singin' the Blues" and "Riverboat Shuffle" that only youth can command, coupled with a sophisticated simplicity and tremendous melodic elegance.

It did not last long. By his mid-twenties, Bix was rarely sober and, although at first his playing remained unaffected, the drink gradually took its toll. It was an era of hard drinking because that was how young people asserted themselves in a land governed by puritans and prohibitionists, but Bix just couldn't stop. He died at age 28.

Bix's first professional publicity photograph, taken in August 1921 in his hometown, Davenport. He later grew a small mustache in an effort to look older and more worldly, but this is the image that has followed his name down the years.

Art Blakey

1919 - 1990

In the nicest possible sense of the term, Art Blakey was the "Godfather." For more than 35 years, his band, the Jazz Messengers, acted as a finishing school for some of the finest young musicians of their day. The list is endless and includes Wynton Marsalis, Wayne Shorter, Lee Morgan, Chick Corea, Freddie Hubbard, Johnny Griffin, and Keith Jarrett—all unknown when he picked them out. Unlike many band-leading drummers, Blakey rarely used the Jazz Messengers as a showcase for his own playing, brilliant though it was. Instead, he took the greatest pleasure in encouraging his young protegés: "Yes, sir, I'm gonna stay with these youngsters. When these get too old I'm gonna get some younger ones. Keeps the mind active!"

People often speculated that Blakey loved working with young people so much because he himself had been orphaned at an early age. He also adopted seven children, in addition to having seven of his own.

Most musicians stayed with him for a couple of years before moving on, but despite the constant changes of personnel, the band's style remained very much the same. The Messengers' music is, as one critic put it, "the definition of hard bop." It is characterized by precise ensemble playing and knife-edge dynamics, with the emphasis on solo improvisation. Blakey's drumming behind his soloists was always a revelation, authoritative but not dictatorial, a wonder of percussive light and shade. His one musical self-indulgence was "Blues March," the witty drum feature composed for him by saxophonist Benny Golson.

Blakey was a great champion for jazz and once outlined his mission as follows: "We started the Messengers because somebody had to mind the store for jazz...It is the only culture that America has brought forth. Everything else comes from another continent. It so happens that jazz comes from black people—and they should know about it, but they know less about it than anybody in the world."

Away from the Messengers, Blakey was one of the most sought-after drummers in jazz. He recorded albums with Sonny Rollins, Milt Jackson, and Cannonball Adderley, among many others, and seemed to have a particular rapport with Thelonious Monk. His special trademarks were a press-roll that gathered force like an impending thunderstorm, and the commanding "snip" of his hi-hat cymbals. On record, his playing is instantly recognizable but, as any drummer will tell you, quite impossible to duplicate.

Any session with Art Blakey in the driving seat was bound to be a success. He had the ability to raise the level of energy and concentration in any musical company and keep it on its toes.

Carla Bley

b. 1938

Her striking looks—the tall, rangy figure and tumbling haystack of reddish blonde hair—have done wonders for Carla Bley's visibility, but she is a remarkable musician in any case. Born Carla Borg in Oakland, California, she played hymns on the piano and sang in church choirs as a child, falling for jazz in a big way at age 17. She moved to New York in 1959, where she worked as a waitress and met and married the pianist Paul Bley. He encouraged her early efforts at composition, and by the end of that year, pieces by "Carla Borg" were being played by leading progressive musicians such as George Russell. Within a few years, now composing full-time under the name Carla Bley, she had become much sought after and her work was recorded by, among others, Charlie Haden, Art Farmer, Jimmy Giuffre, and Gary Burton.

The 1960s proved to be a difficult decade for jazz because its broad popular following had deserted it in favor of rock. Accepting the fact that they were now practicing a minority art, many younger musicians set about building their own support structures and institutions—"making their own scene," as it was often described. One of these was the Jazz Composers' Guild, which put on its own concerts featuring its own orchestra. Carla Bley was a founder member and it was in this context that she developed her distinctive style of jazz-cum-music theater, with works such as *A Genuine Tong Funeral* (subtitled "Dark Opera Without Words") and the vast *Escalator over the Hill*, issued as a triple album in 1971. These are absolutely unmistakable Carla Bley compositions but, like all her mature work, they betray an extraordinary range of influences, from Erik Satie to the Beatles' *Sergeant Pepper*.

Although divorced from Paul Bley in the early 1970s, and remarried to trumpeter Michael Mantler, Bley continued to work under the name by which she was best known. In 1974 she played keyboards in a band led by Jack Bruce, former bassist with the rock band Cream. Since 1976 she has regularly toured with her own bands, playing her own music. The ensembles range from a sextet to the aptly named Very Big Carla Bley Band. In 1985 her opera *Under the Volcano*, based on the novel by Malcolm Lowry, was produced in Los Angeles.

Carla Bley has a great gift for creating memorable melodies, and several of her individual tunes have been adopted as jazz standards, including "Sing Me Softly of the Blues," "Mother of the Dead Man," and "Ad Infinitum."

Carla Bley both conducts and plays keyboards in her own work. Her compositions, with their broad range and memorable tunes, could not be mistaken for anyone else's. Her influence, both as an artist and as an inspired organizer, has been international, extending to Europe and Japan.

Michael Brecker

b. 1949

The tenor saxophone is the leading solo instrument in contemporary jazz, and Michael Brecker is its most influential player of recent times. It is unusual to come across a tenor player below the age of about 35 who does not share Brecker's general approach to jazz.

He has a matchless technique, a fine, centered sound, and an inventiveness that is quite numbing in its speed and scope. He has also perfected a style that allows him to fit into any context. He has recorded with, among others, Paul Simon, Bruce Springsteen, Quincy Jones, John Lennon, and even Frank Sinatra, always sounding exactly right. All these things contribute to his status as an icon among young saxophonists, from London to Tokyo. There are several books of saxophone exercises based on Michael Brecker phrases, and tenor saxophone mouthpieces designed to help in getting the "Brecker sound."

Born in Philadelphia, the son of a jazz-loving, piano-playing attorney, Michael Brecker and his trumpet-playing elder brother, Randy, grew up to the sound of jazz. But they could not ignore the pop and rock music that also surrounded them in their teenage years. The Breckers were among the first generation to be exposed equally to jazz and pop, and they emerged onto the New York scene at the end of the 1960s, exactly the right moment to be in at the start of jazz-rock and fusion. As the Brecker Brothers, they went on to co-lead one of the most popular fusion bands of the 1970s. Michael Brecker went on to play in the even more successful Steps Ahead in the 1980s.

"The rock context meant that you could play complex ideas and not be met by a bunch of puzzled or hostile faces," Michael Brecker recalled. "The rhythm allowed you to communicate and a doorway opened." His own playing certainly bears the residual imprint of saxophonists Junior Walker and King Curtis, along with that of John Coltrane.

Brecker was one of the first to experiment successfully with the EWI (Electronic Wind Instrument), or "windsynth," which harnessed the soundscape of the synthesizer to the mouthpiece and fingering system of the saxophone. The parade of albums under his own name, each obsessively picked over by young tenor players, has been emerging every few years since 1985. Titles include *Now You See It, Now You Don't* (1990), *Tales from the Hudson* (1996), and *Time Is of the Essence* (1999). So far, his albums have netted him seven Grammy Awards.

Michael Brecker's high-energy tenor saxophone style has influenced the playing of a whole generation. His work can be heard on innumerable tracks by star vocalists, as well as on his own albums. Although he was one of the originators of jazz-rock, Brecker's music cannot be confined within a simple category.

Clifford Brown

1 9 3 0 - 1 9 5 6

Clifford Brown first entered a recording studio on March 21, 1952, a 21-year-old member of an obscure Philadelphia rhythm and blues band, Chris Powell's Blue Flames. Four years and one day later, he recorded his final session. Yet in this unbelievably short space of time, he had become one of the most influential trumpet players in jazz. Distinct echoes of his bright, clear-toned style can be heard in the playing of many of today's trumpet giants; for example, players such as Terence Blanchard and Roy Hargrove.

From beginning to end, Brown's records reveal a poised, assured musician with a formidable technique and a vast store of ideas. They are also filled with the energy of youth and stamped with the cheerful good nature that made him universally popular among musicians and fans alike. Sonny Rollins, recalling his friendship with Clifford, summed up the general view: "He was perfect all the way around…a sweet, beautiful individual."

In 1953 Clifford joined Lionel Hampton's big band for a European tour; he was part of a remarkable trumpet section that also included Art Farmer and Quincy Jones. Hampton forbade band members to sit in or record with anyone else during the tour, an instruction that they cheerfully ignored. Clifford was a leading spirit in this rebellion, laying down hours of tape in Swedish and French studios. He would return to his hotel after a gig, retire to his room, and climb straight out of the window and down the fire escape. As it turned out, these nocturnal recordings form a sizeable portion of his total output.

He teamed up with drummer Max Roach in 1954 as co-leader of a quintet. This was when his finest and most mature work was heard. The themes he wrote for the band—"Daahoud," "Joy Spring," "Gertrude's Bounce," and so on—managed to be both catchy and devilishly cunning. Many are still widely played today, their irrepressible perkiness marking them out from the general run of jazz standards. By contrast, his single album with strings, *Clifford Brown with Strings* (1955), a collection of classic ballads, reveals depths of sensitivity and tenderness.

The jazz world loaded Clifford Brown with a great cargo of hope and expectation. Vastly talented, immensely likeable, unencumbered by drugs or unsavory connections, he was the champion who would carry the great jazz tradition into the future. When he was killed, aged 25, in a car crash on the Pennsylvania Turnpike, some of the heart went out of jazz.

Clifford Brown (center) listens intently to a studio playback in August 1954, with (left to right) bassist George Morrow, pianist Richie Powell, and drummer and co-leader Max Roach. The session resulted in the classic album *Brown-Roach Incorporated*. Powell died along with Brown in the car crash on June 26, 1956.

Dave Brubeck

b. 1920

In the late 1950s, Dave Brubeck was a superstar. His quartet toured the world, playing at the largest and most prestigious venues. Brubeck's picture made the front cover of *Time* magazine, and in 1961 the quartet's recording of "Take Five" entered the singles charts, remaining there for 16 weeks and rising to sixth position. Perhaps even more remarkable, "Take Five" has hung around ever afterward as a kind of modern folk tune, played by all manner of characters, including street musicians and even steel bands—despite the fact that the number is in the tricky 5/4 time, which means that a large number of these latter-day performers regularly get it wrong.

Contrary to popular belief, "Take Five" was not Brubeck's own composition, but the work of his alto saxophonist, Paul Desmond. Indeed, Desmond's wispy, ethereal alto is the defining sound of the Dave Brubeck Quartet. The leader's own piano playing, a combination of fiddling intricacy and hysterical crashing about, had its admirers, but the real attraction of the band lay in its presentation. It was aimed initially at a specific and well-defined audience—American college students, who, until the mid-1960s and the advent of the Beatles, considered rock-and-roll beneath them.

Brubeck—with his studious manner, his references to composers such as Hindemith and Milhaud in press interviews, and his musical quotations from Bach—hit exactly the right note for the time. Here was a superior, more intellectual kind of jazz, for superior and intellectual people (like ourselves and our friends). It's a well-tried ploy that often works, but it never worked so well or so thoroughly as with the Dave Brubeck Quartet.

Among Brubeck's most successful records were the album *Jazz at Oberlin* (1953) and *Time Out* (1959), featuring both "Take Five" and "Blue Rondo à la Turk." Brubeck and the quartet won innumerable awards and were invited to the White House several times to perform for visiting heads of state.

Interestingly enough, Brubeck's mass popularity melted away when college kids, deciding it was now all right to like rock, turned toward "progressive" bands such as Cream and Deep Purple. In 1967, Brubeck disbanded the classic quartet to concentrate on composing. The music of his old age is far more attractive and seems more deeply felt. It is full of subtle echoes of old America, of hymns and folk songs, and the sounds of the natural world.

Dave Brubeck playing at a Los Angeles club in the early days, before the formation of his classic quartet. He rarely performed in such informal surroundings once his career took off. The solemnity of the concert hall contributed to the quartet's appeal among the intellectual student audiences of the late 1950s.

Betty Carter

1 9 2 9 - 1 9 9 8

Whatever a jazz singer is—and no two people ever seem to agree on a definition—Betty Carter was one. With her, every performance of a standard popular song was an exercise in demolition and reconstruction. The job was done so thoroughly, and so radically, that faint-hearted listeners gave up in despair, and the rest were left exhausted by the effort of following all the twists and turns of her endlessly inventive imagination.

She started out as Lillie Mae Jones, singing in church in Detroit and eventually studying to become a classical singer at Detroit Conservatory. But she started singing in local clubs and found it more fun. This was the bebop era, and whenever stars such as Charlie Parker or Dizzy Gillespie came to town, she got to sit in with them. Eventually she joined Lionel Hampton's big band. From the very beginning, her formidable willpower was put to the test. Hampton wanted her to sing one way and she was determined to sing another, the bebop way. There would be a row, he would fire her, Hampton's wife, Gladys, would rehire her the next day, and things would continue as before. In the end, Hamp had her billed as "Betty Bebop" and let her do as she liked.

Leaving Hampton in 1951, Betty embarked on a solo career. She met with reasonable success through the fifties, but her greatest admirers tended to be musicians and other singers. Billie Holiday said, "I love her. Betty's five years ahead of her time," which was very flattering but not particularly helpful from a commercial point of view.

Her next break came when Ray Charles, another of her admirers, asked her to join his traveling show and also got her a contract with ABC Records. Their 1961 duet album, *Ray Charles and Betty Carter*, was a great success, but ABC wanted a "girl singing star" and she wanted to be just a singer. They parted company, she tried again with another label, and the same thing happened. Finally she set up her own label, Bet-Car, and nobody could tell her what to do.

Her luck changed almost immediately. In 1979 her Bet-Car album, *The Audience with Betty Carter*, was nominated for a Grammy, she starred at the Newport Jazz Festival, and began the ceaseless round of globetrotting that she kept up almost to the end.

"After me there are no jazz singers," she said, late in life. "It's sad there's nobody stepping on my heels. I don't want it to die with me."

Betty Carter at the height of her powers. She gained control of her own career after many epic battles with managements and record-company executives. She was a dynamic performer, although not in the conventional show-business sense. The excitement in her performance came from the act of musical exploration and discovery.

Charlie Christian

1916 - 1942

Charlie Christian enjoyed the shortest recording career of any major jazz musician—less than two years—yet his influence has been incalculable. Today, more than half a century after his death at age 25, his sound continues to haunt the electric guitar in jazz.

The guitar is a naturally quiet instrument. Musicians had been experimenting for years with ways of making it loud enough to be heard properly in a band, but it wasn't until 1937 that a practical method was found and the first commercial electric guitar, the Gibson ES-150, came onto the market. As it turned out, the addition of an electromagnetic pickup produced not just a louder guitar but what was effectively a new instrument. When playing single notes, it sounded more like a tenor saxophone than anything else. The 21-year-old Charlie Christian instantly grasped this fact. Indeed, he had been conducting his own experiments in an attempt to create exactly this sound.

It was a sublime accident that the newly invented instrument found an improviser of near genius as its first prominent player. Charlie's solo lines curled and folded with deceptive ease—a cool, measured narrative, amazingly mature for one of his years. Everyone who heard him was struck by the stylistic similarity with saxophonist Lester Young. On the few recordings where they appear together, they sound just like brothers.

Charlie's short career in the limelight was passed with Benny Goodman's band, and the recording of his feature number, "Solo Flight," catches the essence of his style to perfection. Away from the band, he regularly attended jam sessions at Minton's Playhouse, the Harlem after-hours club where the beginnings of bebop were hatched. He was so popular there that Minton's boss, Teddy Hill, installed an amplifier on stage to save Charlie the trouble of bringing his own. A handful of amateur recordings made there in 1941 show how wonderfully expansive Charlie's playing could be when he was freed from time restrictions. Interestingly, there is no hint of bebop phraseology in these solos. Like Lester, Charlie never tired of swing.

But already his health was deteriorating. His new, hectic life roused the tuberculosis that had lain dormant in him since childhood. Sent to a sanitorium on Staten Island, he began to make a partial recovery, but the boredom was getting him down. One night he slipped out with some friends for an evening's fun, caught a chill, and died.

Charlie Christian, aged about 24, during his brief career with Benny Goodman's band. This shot was probably taken before or after a show because he is sitting at a trumpet-section desk and picking the guitar finger-style, not using a plectrum.

Nat "King" Cole

1917 - 1965

In his mammoth academic book *The Swing Era*, musicologist Gunther Schuller calls Nat Cole "not only one of the most outstanding pianists of his day [the 1940s] but stylistically one of the most advanced." He further claims that for a few years Nat's band, the King Cole Trio, was harmonically ahead of everyone, even Charlie Parker. Nat recorded with Lester Young and Lionel Hampton, toured as a star soloist with Jazz at the Philharmonic, and was widely tipped as successor to his idol, Earl Hines.

The Trio was one of the most imitated bands in the world in the late 1940s, particularly in its style of presentation—three cool cats huddled around a white baby grand piano, sharp and snappy, processed hair and big smiles, delivering hip messages: "Hit That Jive, Jack!," "Straighten Up and Fly Right!" They had their own radio show and won all the major U.S. music polls, with Nat himself topping the jazz piano category.

Jazz posterity never quite forgave Nat for turning his back on all this in favor of the black tie, the spotlight, and sweet strings in the background. But it was inevitable. Once that soft, warm, lingering voice began to work its magic, there could be no doubt that Nat Cole was a man born for the American song. It's surprising, in fact, that the process took so long. Nat recorded his first ballad in 1941, and the Trio's repertoire was full of them. He took leave of the Trio, and eventually the piano, reluctantly and with infinite regret. It wasn't until 1955 that he finally made the complete break. It is widely believed that his wife, Maria, was responsible for Nat abandoning the last vestiges of the trio format.

It was once fashionable to interpret Nat Cole's career as a capitulation—"selling out to the white establishment" and all that. In fact, the opposite is true. In those days, the easiest way for a black entertainer to succeed was by conforming to racial stereotype. Black artists such as Louis Jordan and Cab Calloway got along fine because they performed the way white people expected them to perform. It was the same right across show business, from Bojangles to Billie Holiday. A careful distance was maintained.

One thing black artists didn't do, and that was to speak intimately to everyone, reminding them of their shared humanity. Until, that is, Nat Cole came along. He sang romantic ballads with such moving simplicity that he became not a great *black* singer, but a great *American* singer.

Nat "King" Cole at a Capitol recording session. Although he had the services of the best arrangers and conductors in the business, Nat took an active role in directing his own sessions. As well as having vast experience as a band leader, he also possessed the gift of perfect pitch.

Ornette Coleman

b. 1930

The usual objection raised among jazz listeners when a new and puzzling development takes place is to denounce it as not being jazz at all. But when Ornette Coleman's first recordings appeared, toward the end of the 1950s, this objection was ruled out from the start. It plainly was jazz in all essential respects and, superficially at least, Coleman's sound, and even his tunes, bore some resemblance to Charlie Parker's. But when you listened carefully, there was something disturbingly odd about it all.

Parker would play the theme, construct his solos on the chord sequence thus established, and end with the theme again. Coleman didn't do this. In his solos he pursued melodic ideas regardless of their relationship to any underlying harmony. He soon dropped the piano from his band because the chords it played had become irrelevant.

Coleman was no experimenter. He was not pursuing some laboriously worked-out theory. He had actually been playing this way for years, and been roundly abused for his pains. Most of his work had been in rhythm and blues bands, whose audiences knew exactly what they wanted, and it certainly wasn't that. No, Ornette Coleman, like Parker before him, seemed to be driven by a compulsion, some kind of personal demon that he was powerless to control.

The titles of Coleman's early albums emphasized the revolutionary nature of his music: *Tomorrow Is the Question!* (1959), *Change of the Century* (1959), *The Shape of Jazz to Come* (1959). The extent to which listeners accepted the music depended largely upon what they enjoyed about jazz in the first place. Those attracted by the iconoclastic, anti-establishment, self-expressive approach welcomed Coleman warmly. Those who valued subtle swing, intimacy, and understated wit couldn't take him at any price. The same thing had happened with bebop, back in the forties, but most people had eventually come round to accepting bop once they got used to the idiom. In Coleman's case, this never really happened. A great divide seemed to open, separating the avant-garde from the rest.

Coleman went on to lead a trio, in which he also played trumpet and violin (both very unconventionally), and the electric band Prime Time. He also developed a theory of music, which he dubbed "harmolodics," based on a concept of harmony, not as static chords but as a series of interweaving lines. His ideas have had a huge influence on later developments in jazz.

This publicity shot of Ornette Coleman, taken in the early 1960s, attempts to display all his unique musical talents. Although primarily known as an alto saxophone player and composer, he also studied trumpet and violin for two years before playing them in a trio he formed in 1965.

John Coltrane

1 9 2 6 - 1 9 6 7

The most influential jazz musician since Charlie Parker, Coltrane continues to cast a giant shadow more than three decades after his death. His classic quartet records, made between 1961 and 1965, with McCoy Tyner on piano and Elvin Jones on drums, set a pattern for small-band jazz that is still largely adhered to.

When he first emerged into the limelight, with the Miles Davis Quintet in 1955, Coltrane's saxophone playing was greeted with consternation. His metallic, unyielding tone and angular phrases struck many listeners as deliberately ugly. But there was an intensity and high seriousness about his whole presentation and demeanor that made people listen.

There is little doubt that Coltrane was capable of single-mindedness bordering on obsession. He cured himself of heroin addiction by sheer willpower, practiced eight hours a day, and was never satisfied until he had worked through every possible alteration and substitution in a chord sequence. Not surprisingly, he was somewhat lacking in a sense of humor, but was capable of great delicacy and tenderness on occasion, as his album *Ballads* (1962) shows. More typical are *Giant Steps* (1959; its title tune is still a test piece for improvisers), *Africa/Brass* (1961; with its wonderful evocation of untamed vastness), and *A Love Supreme* (1964; Coltrane's masterpiece, following his religious conversion).

Coltrane's technical mastery of the saxophone allowed him to play passages at such blinding speed that the notes seemed to merge into one another, an effect famously described as "sheets of sound." Allied to his use of modes and scales as a basis for improvisation, and his habit of producing immensely long solos, it gave his playing an awesome grandeur. The trouble was that, in lesser hands, the same approach could, and did, result in stupendous levels of boredom. As Dr. Johnson said of the poet Milton: "Like other heroes, he is to be admired rather than imitated."

One of Coltrane's notable achievements was to revive the fortunes of the soprano saxophone, previously regarded as virtually the sole property of Sidney Bechet. From 1959 (the year of Bechet's death, incidentally), Coltrane employed the soprano as his second instrument, producing on it a plaintive, reedy tone, reminiscent of some Eastern wind instrument. Others followed his lead, and the soprano is now the accepted "double" of many tenor players.

At the time of his death, Coltrane had abandoned the quartet format and was immersed in somewhat inconclusive experiments with free jazz.

John Coltrane, pictured in the early 1960s, at the time of his classic quartet recordings. The pose is completely typical. His embouchure (grip on the mouthpiece) could have come straight out of a saxophone textbook.

Eddie Condon

1905 - 1973

The name of Eddie Condon comes complete with the image of a dapper figure in a bow tie, the words "Chicago jazz," a bottle of Scotch, and a string of wisecracks.

Chicago was the city where, in the 1920s, the great New Orleans jazz masters settled to work and to make records. It was here, too, that jazz picked up its first sizeable body of young white adherents and musical apprentices. Condon, a banjo and guitar player, was a leading spirit among them. His circle included all the great names identified with the fiery, loose-knit music that went under the heading "Chicago style"—such as saxophonist Bud Freeman, clarinetist Frank Teschemacher, cornetist Jimmy McPartland, and singer and entrepreneur Red McKenzie. These days are vividly recalled in Condon's autobiography, *We Called It Music: a Generation of Jazz* (1947), one of the most hilariously readable books ever written by a jazz musician.

Eddie was a good rhythm guitarist, but his greatest talent was for organizing sessions, running his New York club (motto: "We never throw anyone out, and we never throw anyone in"), and simply being Eddie Condon. This entailed living up to his reputation as a drinker on an epic scale, although, like Dean Martin and other famous imbibers, he didn't drink as much as he pretended to. He always went on the wagon for a few weeks in the summer to get in shape for his annual life-insurance examination. Also, unlike genuine drunks, he was always impeccably turned out—newly pressed suit, freshly laundered shirt, neat bow tie, and not a hair out of place. Nor was his wit ever blunted by drink.

But he did spend a lot of time at the bar. Before he had his own place, he worked with Joe Marsala's band at the Hickory House. One day the proprietor said to Marsala: "Joe, there's a guy over there who must really love your music. He's in here every night at the bar." "Jack," replied Marsala, "that's Eddie Condon. You're paying his salary." When asked for his favorite recipe for a hangover cure, Condon began, "Take the juice of two quarts of whisky…" In an effort to discourage his drinking, his wife, Phyllis, drew up a list of famous musicians who had died of liver disease. Eddie read the list thoughtfully and handed it back. "We're short of a drummer," he observed.

Condon's devotion to his style of music was absolute, and he hated all aspects of modernism in jazz. Once, when a waiter dropped a tray of plates and cutlery, he yelled out, "We don't want any of that progressive jazz in here!"

The dapper Eddie Condon playing at the New York club that bore his name. His very appearance, with bow tie and neatly parted hair, recalled the Roaring Twenties of his youth. Condon always played a four-string guitar, a type originally introduced to enable banjo players to "double" on guitar.

Chick Corea

b. 1941

Chick Corea was a child prodigy. He was born in Chelsea, Massachusetts, began playing piano at the age of four, and took up the drums at age eight. He originally came to prominence as a Latin-style pianist, first with Mongo Santamaria, then Willie Bobo and Herbie Mann. However, he soon escaped into jazz proper, making his first big impression on Stan Getz's 1967 album, *Sweet Rain*. He also recorded a well-received solo album, *Now He Sings, Now He Sobs* (1968). But it was his work (along with Herbie Hancock and Keith Jarrett) on Miles Davis's revolutionary series of early fusion albums, from *Filles de Kilimanjaro* (1968) to *Live-Evil* (1970), that made him an international star. This was the time when jazz pianists everywhere were struggling to come to grips with electric keyboards, and Corea's delicate use of the Fender-Rhodes electric piano set the standard to be emulated.

Leaving Miles in 1970, he got together with bassist Dave Holland, drummer Barry Altschul, and multi-reed player Anthony Braxton to form Circle. This band's severely abstract music attracted a following, especially in Europe, and it recorded several albums, but it was performing almost exclusively to audiences of keen, specialist fans. Corea eventually became dissatisfied with this situation and left rather abruptly in late 1971.

His change of heart may have had something to do with the fact that he was beginning to study Scientology, and was reassessing his life in the process. He remained an adherent of the Church of Scientology from then onward, and in the 1990s, found himself barred from playing in Germany, where Scientology is banned as an undesirable cult. Certainly, there could be no greater contrast than between Circle and his next band, the delightfully melodic Return to Forever, featuring the singer Flora Purim, percussionist Airto Moreira, and saxophonist and flautist Joe Farrell.

This band lasted for a decade, although it went through three complete changes of personnel, becoming heavier and less distinctive each time. Players who passed through Return to Forever over this period included such fusion stars as guitarist Al Di Meola, pianist Lenny White, and drummer Steve Gadd.

By the end of the 1970s, Corea was growing dissatisfied with the electric keyboard. He returned to the acoustic piano and undertook world tours, first playing duets with pianist Herbie Hancock and later with vibraphonist Gary Burton. Eventually, he settled on alternating between two contrasting groups, his Akoustic and Elektric bands.

As both a pianist and composer, Chick Corea's importance in contemporary jazz is on a par with that of Herbie Hancock and Keith Jarrett. His compositions include such modern jazz standards as "La Fiesta" and "Spain."

Miles Davis

1 9 2 6 - 1 9 9 1

Not being allowed to hold hereditary titles, American men who are keen to emphasize their proud lineage add Roman numerals after their names. Step forward Miles Dewey Davis III. Miles the First owned 500 acres of Arkansas, the first black landowner in the state. Miles the Second was a successful dentist and breeder of racehorses. Miles the Third was a good, but by no means momentous, bebop trumpeter who turned himself into one of the great jazz voices.

It was made plain to Miles III from his earliest years that the Davises had succeeded in a hostile world by being smart, tough, and quick to avenge any slur upon their dignity. Above all, it was vital to take the initiative, to be in command of every situation, and never to betray a glimmer of self-doubt.

But along with this came a rare capacity for self-scrutiny. At a remarkably early age, Miles examined his own playing and worked out that his true talent lay in a kind of dramatic understatement. Methodically, he set about developing this, and one can follow the process through his records, made over four decades. At the age of 19, he sought out saxophonist Charlie Parker in order to learn from him, and became a member of Parker's classic quintet of the late 1940s.

Davis was always surrounded by the greatest players of the day, but somehow the ear is drawn to the exquisite, polished simplicity of his own utterances. Beginning with the nine-piece Birth of the Cool band in 1948–49, through the famous quintet of the 1950s (featuring John Coltrane), the revolutionary *Kind of Blue* album (1959), the monumental recordings accompanied by Gil Evans's 20-piece orchestra, the pioneering second quintet of the 1960s (with Herbie Hancock and Wayne Shorter), to the jazz-fusion of the 1970s and outright funk of his last years, Miles Davis was at the forefront.

At any stage in this progress, a more timid man would have stopped, happy to have found a successful formula and eager to exploit it. But once other people grasped the elements of his new style well enough to start imitating it, Miles changed direction. This applies not only to his music but also to his visual style. He was always the epitome of chic. In the late 1940s, he wore zoot suits, Mr. B shirt collars, and painted ties; in the 1950s, it was an Ivy League suit or silk dinner jacket; in the 1960s, chinos and Italian sweaters, then kaftans; and in his last years, a bizarre selection of baggy, street-cred outfits.

In short, Miles Davis was, quite simply, the ultimate jazz icon.

The magnetism and sheer force of character that made Miles Davis a jazz icon comes over strongly in this late picture. He overcame a brief heroin habit by willpower alone, suffered a number of quite serious illnesses, and once almost died in a car crash. He fought back every time.

Eric Dolphy

1 9 2 8 - 1 9 6 4

Like Charlie Christian, Clifford Brown, and other jazz innovators who died young, Eric Dolphy left quite a small body of recorded work but continues to exert a considerable influence to this day. In his case, this has a lot to do with his versatility. He was an equally impressive performer on alto saxophone, clarinet, bass clarinet, and flute. Indeed, on the last two instruments, he was the first soloist of real distinction.

Stylistically, Dolphy's music belongs to the era of Ornette Coleman and John Coltrane, but sounds more traditionally based than either of them. He liked to work within the same confines as Charlie Parker—the 32-bar song and 12-bar blues—but his approach was looser and freer. For this reason, many listeners found their way into the enjoyment of free jazz through listening to Dolphy—there was something familiar to hang onto. By the same token, later generations of players have tended to follow Dolphy's flexible approach in preference to the all-out free improvisation of the 1960s avant-garde.

But quite apart from his influence on others, Dolphy was a delightful player in his own right. There is a great deal of wit and simple good humor in his improvisations, especially on bass clarinet. He gives the big instrument a distinct personality, burbling and chuckling away in a quite irresistible manner. His flute style, too, is unlike anyone else's, full of windy cries and twittering birdcalls.

It may be significant that Dolphy was born and grew up in Los Angeles, far from the hard-bop nurseries of New York, Philadelphia, and Detroit. The jazz feeling on the West Coast was always lighter. His first big-time job was with the popular Chico Hamilton Quintet, which included a cello in its lineup. He did not move to New York until he was 30, when he worked with Charles Mingus, Max Roach, and George Russell.

In 1961 he briefly led his own quintet, which included the trumpeter Booker Little, before making a solo tour in Europe. He spent the first few months of 1962 as an additional member of John Coltrane's quartet. But Dolphy was a freelance player at heart and loved the challenge of new players and new surroundings. He died in Berlin, of undiagnosed diabetes, a few days after his 36th birthday.

Eric Dolphy made a surprising number of recordings in his short musical career. Among the best are his contributions to several Mingus albums and his live recordings in Europe. His masterpiece is, however, undoubtedly the Blue Note album *Out to Lunch* (1964).

Eric Dolphy is pictured here with a bass clarinet. His mastery of this awkward instrument is unrivaled in jazz, and his playing gave it a distinct character. The same is true of his work on flute and alto saxophone.

Roy Eldridge

1 9 1 1 - 1 9 8 9

In jazz trumpet history, Roy "Little Jazz" Eldridge provides the link between Louis Armstrong and Dizzy Gillespie. He was a bustling, whole-hearted man, full of energy and spirit, and his playing reflected his character to perfection. It comes as no surprise to learn that Roy's early heroes included several saxophone players, such as Benny Carter, because they played so many more notes than the trumpeters of the day. To play as much as possible, covering as great a range as possible, was his ambition. For a while, in the late 1930s and early 1940s, he was the fastest trumpet player in jazz.

Roy led his own band at the famous Three Deuces, on New York's 52nd Street, and later at the Arcadia Ballroom, before joining Gene Krupa's band in 1941. With Krupa, Roy became a star, with his dazzling trumpet features and humorous vocal duets with Anita O'Day, the band's singer. But racism permeated American society at that time and racially mixed bands were almost unheard of. Traveling with a white band proved to be a nightmare for Eldridge, despite the support of his fellow musicians, and he eventually left. A similar experience with Artie Shaw's orchestra soon afterward caused him to vow never to join another white band. Later, in 1950, he wrote an impassioned article entitled "Jim Crow Is Killing Jazz" for the magazine *Negro Digest*.

In 1944 Eldridge formed his own big band, which failed. He picked himself up and tried again in 1946, but bands were collapsing all around and Eldridge's second attempt was an even bigger disaster than the first. He went back to freelance playing, only to discover after a year or so that bebop was advancing and his former disciple, Dizzy Gillespie, had supplanted him as the fastest, highest trumpet player alive.

In 1950 Eldridge took himself off to France, where the adulation of French audiences restored his ruffled self-confidence. Returning home a year later, he found that swing players of his generation were being acknowledged once more, and began recording and performing with all-star groups, along with Coleman Hawkins, Johnny Hodges, Ella Fitzgerald, and the Jazz at the Philharmonic company. This was when his finest mature work was recorded, in particular the albums *The Strolling Mr. Eldridge* (1954) and *At the Opera House* (1957), with Coleman Hawkins. There were also some fiery, combative, but essentially good-natured reunions with Dizzy during those years.

Roy Eldridge in his mature heyday. An exuberant character, he enlivened the backstage life of every band he played with. On several occasions, it's recounted, he became so engrossed in telling jokes and stories that he forgot when it was his turn to take a solo.

Duke Ellington

1899 - 1974

The whole world knows that Edward Kennedy Ellington is the greatest jazz composer, but it is now widely accepted that he is numbered among the greatest composers of the 20th century. To use one of his own phrases, his music is "beyond category." However you define jazz, Ellington consistently went beyond it. His large-scale works, such as *Black, Brown and Beige* (1943) and *Harlem (A Tone Parallel to Harlem)* (1950), his concert suites, and the oratorios called "Sacred Concerts" would not fit most people's definitions, but they could not have been written by anyone else—which is to say anyone but the man who also wrote "Ko-Ko" and "Cotton Tail."

And none of it would have existed without that other miraculous creation, his band—or, to give it its proper, dignified title, Duke Ellington and his Famous Orchestra. He assembled this mighty, many-voiced instrument over the years, each player chosen for the particular quality Ellington sensed that player could contribute. As players left and others joined, so the band's sound changed subtly, but the overall effect remained the same. It was like the sound of an enormous human voice, broad and full-throated. There has been nothing like it before or since. Each individual voice in the ensemble is recognizable: Johnny Hodges, Cootie Williams, Harry Carney, Joe Nanton (known to all as "Tricky Sam"), and the rest. On record it is magnificent; in the flesh it was simply overwhelming.

Perhaps the most amazing thing about Ellington's art is its genesis and growth. He began, after a few false starts, in 1927 by landing the job of band leader at the Cotton Club, in Harlem. This was a white nightclub in a black ghetto, with a floor show featuring jungles, tropical thunderstorms, natives dancing round cooking pots, and dusky maidens dressed in nothing very much. Ellington, an extremely presentable, well-spoken, middle-class young man from Washington, D.C., was handed the task of producing suitable music to accompany this unedifying spectacle.

He came up with a series of pieces that brought together instrumental textures and tone colors in quite unprecedented combinations. The growls and barks, the mysterious chantings and sudden flutterings of the nightclub jungle remained a part of his vocabulary for the rest of his life. From the tourist confection of *Jungle Nights in Harlem* (1930) to the deep spirituality of the *Second Sacred Concert* (1968), the same imagination was at work, using essentially the same materials.

Ellington in his backstage dressing-room, sometime in the late 1940s. The packed wardrobe rail visible behind him bears testimony to his concern always to be fashionably and immaculately dressed. He traveled with at least a dozen suits and innumerable shirts, each bearing his monogram. A valet was always in attendance.

Bill Evans

Subtlety is the basis of Bill Evans's music. The pale, shifting tone colors of his piano improvisations grow more fascinating the more closely one listens to them. The more acute one's ear, the more enjoyment one will derive because, although he normally took classic American songs as a basis, the tune was only the starting point.

Evans's first album came out in 1957, when he was 28 years old and completely unknown. Although it made very little public impact, Miles Davis heard it and offered him the piano chair in his quintet. This was the time when Miles was working on the modal experiments that resulted in the landmark album *Kind of Blue* (1959), and the album made Evans's reputation. In fact, *Kind of Blue* owes much of its atmosphere to his sparse, delicate chords and restrained manner.

Leaving Miles after nine months, Evans formed the trio that was to be his main working context for the rest of his life. This was by no means a one-man band of star pianist and bass-drums accompaniment. Together with his remarkable bassist, Scott LaFaro, Evans evolved a style in which the bass became an equal melodic voice instead of simply a timekeeper. This had only recently become possible with the invention of a reliable amplifier for the double bass, and still the trio could work effectively only in concert halls or very quiet jazz clubs. When LaFaro died in a road accident in 1961, Evans had to stop working until he could find another player with a similar approach and an equivalent technique. It was some months before he finally located Chuck Israels. He was followed in turn by Gary Peacock and Eddie Gomez. The trio's drummer throughout most of its life was the highly sensitive Paul Motian.

The subdued nature of Bill Evans's music was not universally appreciated, and several critics wondered whether, especially in slow ballad improvisations, he had strayed over the boundary between jazz piano and the late romanticism of composers such as Debussy and Ravel. Today, however, he is widely imitated, and his importance in jazz can be judged by the amount of Bill Evans to be found in the playing of virtually every important contemporary pianist, including Keith Jarrett and Herbie Hancock.

Several of his compositions have become minor jazz standards, in particular "Turn Out the Stars" and "Waltz for Debby," and his "Blue in Green" (originally credited to Miles Davis) is a classic by virtue of its presence on *Kind of Blue*.

Even on the concert platform, Bill Evans, the pianists' pianist, gave the impression that he was playing purely for himself. He sat with his head bowed low over the keyboard, listening intently to the balance and timbre of each chord, and seemed to disappear into the music.

Ella Fitzgerald

1917 - 1996

Think of all the qualities you look for in a great popular singer's voice—warmth, intimacy, expressiveness. Think, above all, of that indefinable sense that the voice belongs to someone you immediately feel at home with, and you will find it in full bloom whenever you hear Ella Fitzgerald. It was an ageless voice. It seems to have settled down, some time in her late twenties, into a mellow smoothness and simply stayed that way, so that she was at or near her peak from the end of World War II until at least the mid-1970s.

There were two sides to her singing—the serene, creamy style of her famous *Songbook* albums of the 1950s and early 1960s, and the scatting, swing-into-bebop that she delighted to let loose in jazz-friendly surroundings. She was, in fact, a painfully shy and withdrawn woman, ill at ease with strangers and nervous of showing her true feelings about anything. But music seemed to turn on an inner light, transforming her into a lively, outgoing person for as long as the song lasted.

Above: Duke Ellington captivated by Ella's performance at a New York nightclub in 1948. Benny Goodman sits just behind him.

The official story of her early life tells the usual fairytale of the nervous young girl, persuaded to enter a talent contest, spotted by a famous band leader (Chick Webb, in her case), and raised to instant stardom. What it doesn't tell is everything else. She won the talent contest, but was denied the prize of a week's engagement at the Apollo Theater because she was a vagrant, a homeless teenager—dirty, smelly, unkempt, and surviving on semicriminal activities. Webb was impressed with her singing, but had to be persuaded to take her on because she looked so unpresentable. Once she had cleaned up, however, and stood up in front of Webb's band at the Savoy Ballroom, she created a sensation.

All her dozens of recordings with Webb are lively "rhythm numbers," and they were so successful that when Webb died suddenly in 1939, the band carried on for a couple of years as Ella Fitzgerald and Her Orchestra. In later life, when she was acknowledged as one of the greatest vocalists in the history of American song, it was usually swing tunes that brought out the best in her.

Left: Ella photographed in the 1950s, during the era of her triumphant series of *Songbook* recordings. Even Cole Porter, who disliked jazz, heaped praise on her interpretations of his songs.

Slim Gaillard

1916 - 1991

A man who could speak at least six languages, and still invent one of his own. A man who had a hit record with a song about a cement mixer. A man whose philosophy included the important dictum: "Don't worry if your clock is wrong; it's the right time somewhere." A man who could play piano with his knuckles. This was a man to be reckoned with. This was Bulee "Slim" Gaillard, and to tell the full story of his eventful life would take up this entire book.

He was born in Cuba to a black Cuban mother and German-Jewish father (two languages). A cabin boy, he was stranded in Crete at age 12, worked on Mediterranean tramp steamers (two more languages), finally got to Detroit, and was taken in by an Armenian family (another two languages). He won a talent contest as a tap-dancer, taught himself guitar and piano, and teamed up with bassist Slam Stewart. As a hip, zany act called Slim and Slam, they had a monster hit in 1938 with "Flat Foot Floogie." When he was drafted into the U.S. Army in 1942, it was discovered that Slim had an IQ in excess of 130. He became one of the few black American bomber pilots of World War II, and was invalided out in 1944 with the rank of captain and a body peppered with shrapnel.

Settling in Los Angeles, Slim became the court jester of bebop, the epitome of hipness for the Hollywood smart set, who copied the garbled private language he called "Vout." No conversation could possibly be considered hip without a scattering of Vout words, such as "oroonie" and "oreenie." For instance, in Vout, "Dizzy Gillespie" became "Daz McSkivens Vouts Oroonie."

Slim recorded one session with both Dizzy and Charlie Parker in 1945. This was also the year of his worldwide hit song, "Cement Mixer." Other great works included "Chicken Rhythm," "The Groove Juice Special," and "Sploghm!"

When fashions changed, Slim vanished. Many thought he was dead, but he wasn't. He grew a beard and became an actor. He appeared in *Mission Impossible*, *Charlie's Angels*, *Roots*, and (totally encased in a gorilla costume) *Planet of the Apes*. He also owned a fruit farm. In 1982 Slim went to Europe, liked it, and settled in London. There he became a celebrity all over again, turning up not only in jazz clubs but also on radio chat shows, quizzes, and even poetry programs. As well as that, he was Marvin Gaye's father-in-law.

"They say I'm an historic figure," Slim reflected toward the end of his life. "I don't say it, I let them say it."

As a young man in Hollywood, Slim was so handsome that he had the nickname "Dark Gable." He stayed good-looking to the end, in a roguish kind of way. His beret (always white or scarlet) was regularly seen at the Chelsea Arts Club in London, of which he was a valued member.

Jan Garbarek

b. 1947

Nothing could better illustrate the way jazz has spread to become a worldwide musical language, assimilating other idioms as it goes, than the career of the Norwegian saxophonist and composer Jan Garbarek. He began conventionally enough, picking up on John Coltrane as a teenager and learning through imitation. By his early twenties, Garbarek was one of Europe's most promising young players, still very much in the shadow of Coltrane. Soon, however, a more personal style began to emerge. The tone became lighter and clearer, the phrasing more restrained. At the same time, he was turning increasingly to his own heritage of Nordic folk music for material.

As it developed through the 1970s and 1980s into the 1990s, Garbarek's music moved farther and farther from the jazz mainstream and into the Nordic twilight. Terms such as "chilly" and "severe" were commonly employed to describe its effect, but no-one could deny its pale beauty. Yet Garbarek didn't stop there. He found that his high, keening tone would fit into almost any context, and was soon recording with the Latin percussionist Nana Vasconcelos, the Pakistani singer Usted Fateh Ali Khan, and other unlikely partners. He brought together ethnic music, medieval plainsong, electronics, composition, and improvisation to create what could only be described as "Garbarek music."

None of this would have been possible in the conventional world of jazz promotion and recording. Together with many other European musicians, Garbarek owes a great deal to Manfred Eicher—a man of energy, enterprise, and unique taste—and his record label, ECM. An ECM album, and later CD, constituted a complete work. The austere black-and-white cover photograph, the notes reduced to essential information, the clean simplicity of the sound—all these complemented the music. "The most beautiful sound next to silence," is how he once described his ideal. The "rough and bombastic" side of jazz held little appeal for Eicher. He was interested in capturing "music that gets to you slowly," in the manner of chamber music.

Happily, the public caught up with Eicher's rarefied tastes, and in the 1990s the concepts of minimalism, pioneered in music by Philip Glass and Terry Riley, and of "ambient music," first explored by Brian Eno and others, became widely accepted. As a result, Garbarek found himself a much sought-after international artist, to the extent of appearing briefly, in 1996, in the British album charts with his ECM disc *Visible World*.

Jan Garbarek pioneered a distinctively Nordic approach to jazz over the course of a quarter of a century, encouraged by the visionary German record producer Manfred Eicher and his ECM label.

Erroll Garner

1 9 2 1 - 1 9 7 7

Erroll Garner played piano like a one-man big band. His left hand, steadily chugging away, was the rhythm section; his right supplied the brass and saxophones. Once heard, his playing could never be mistaken for anyone else's.

Garner was a kindly, good-natured man who enjoyed cooking and entertaining. He had been born a twin, his brother being severely handicapped, and he sometimes mused aloud about the unfairness of this. Music came so easily to him that he never had to work at it. He was ambidextrous and had perfect pitch. He never studied, never practiced methodically, never even bothered learning how to read music. He simply sat down at the piano and played whatever came into his head.

Usually, the music came out in one of two styles: bright swing or lush ballad. On swing numbers he made a point of playing off the steady beat of his left hand against righthand phrases so exaggeratedly behind the beat that the whole thing sometimes turned into delighted self-parody.

Similarly, his slow ballads often developed into huge, elaborate canvases, with every nook and cranny covered in decoration, until it became so over-the-top that the only response was a knowing smile. Erroll was the first to see the joke. A favorite Garner trick was the keep-'em-guessing introduction, often employed at concerts. These could go on for minutes on end, with all kinds of misleading hints, until the tune came tripping out, like a conjurer's white rabbit, to storms of applause. Several vintage examples occur on his hugely popular album *Concert by the Sea* (1955).

Most great stylists in jazz have their acolytes and imitators, but Erroll Garner was just too eccentric to provide a good model. In any case, his technique was so unorthodox that most trained pianists hadn't the first clue how he did it. One exception was Dudley Moore, whose devotion was so fanatical that he carried a manuscript book with him to film locations, filling the empty hours by transcribing Garner's records.

Despite his lack of formal training, Garner composed a number of very attractive, impressionistic piano pieces, including "Turquoise," "Pastel," and, most famously, "Misty." He had the same broad popular appeal as Louis Armstrong. His music was enjoyed far beyond the limited circle of jazz lovers, and although he rarely spoke directly to his audiences, he radiated enjoyment and a kind of elfin charm.

Erroll Garner's mischievous grin matched the playful good humor of his music. In this picture his bassist, Eddie Calhoun, listening intently, seems to be having the usual trouble guessing what Erroll will do next.

Stan Getz

1 9 2 7 - 1 9 9 1

One note is all it takes. The melting beauty of Stan Getz's tone is so distinctive that it could never be mistaken for anyone else's. And yet the sound itself changed quite radically over the course of his 45-year career, gradually evolving from the delicate lightness of his youth to the broad, almost operatic proportions of his last few years.

Getz's whole approach to the tenor saxophone grew out of his lifelong love for the playing of Lester Young. He was not alone in this. Most tenor players of his generation had been captivated as teenagers by the light, mercurial sound and elusive simplicity of Lester's solos with the Count Basie band during the late 1930s and early 1940s. It was among these disciples of Lester that the word "cool" first came to be used as a term of approval.

The jazz world began paying serious attention to Stan Getz in 1949, with the release of "Early Autumn," his feature number with Woody Herman's band, of which he was then a member. The tone is so light that the notes evaporate as they emerge, like breath on a frosty morning. Over the next few years, Getz produced a long series of records with his own quartets and quintets, consisting mainly of pale, watercolor impressions of standard songs, exquisite in their delicacy. Quite soon, however, the sound acquired a new, steely edge and Getz's up-tempo numbers generated formidable energy and drive.

The really big change occurred in 1961, at a time when the cool sound was no longer fashionable and Getz's fortunes were at a low ebb. The album that signaled the change was *Focus* (1961), featuring Getz with a double string quartet and rhythm section, and often cited as his masterpiece. In these surroundings, the sound blossomed, and it continued to grow like some luxuriant, exotic plant throughout the rest of his life. The following year he recorded an album, *Jazz Samba* (1962), in the newly fashionable style, imported from Brazil, known as bossa nova. A single taken from the album entered the charts, soon followed by an even bigger hit, "The Girl from Ipanema," with vocalist Astrud Gilberto.

Some of Getz's finest playing is preserved on his bossa nova albums, but unwilling to become trapped in a formula, he moved on, working mainly in his favorite format, the tenor-and-rhythm quartet. The albums of his final years, such as *Serenity* (1987), with rhythm section led by pianist Kenny Barron, and *The Dolphin* (1981), with pianist Lou Levy, are among the best of all.

Stan Getz, aged 22, pictured here at a Metronome All-Stars session in 1949, his first year in the spotlight following his spectacular success on Woody Herman's "Early Autumn." His boyish good looks betray no hint of the drug addiction that had already taken hold and that would dog him for the rest of his life.

Dizzy Gillespie

1917 - 1993

Dizzy was the smiling bebopper. This was in addition, of course, to his phenomenal powers as a trumpeter and improviser, but his buoyant and cheerful personality was a great asset. It kept him afloat in the early days, when his contemporaries and colleagues, such as Charlie Parker, were struggling against public hostility, and it made him almost the only major jazz figure of his generation never to touch hard drugs. He certainly outlived almost all of them.

Gillespie's little eccentricities—his beret and goatee beard and, later on, his trumpet with its bell tilted at 45 degrees—made him a highly visible character, but he was as rigorous a musician as any, and a born leader. The big band that he formed in the late 1940s played music so ferocious that *Time* magazine was moved to denounce it in an article entitled "How Deaf Can You Get?," but Dizzy's amiable clowning kept the band alive while big bands were folding up all around, including many of the biggest names.

Ten years later, public taste had advanced and Dizzy had calmed down somewhat, perhaps under the influence of the Bahai faith, which he had enthusiastically adopted. He was judged reliable enough to be sent abroad as a cultural ambassador, leading a big band financed by the U.S. State Department. The experience of dealing with government agencies convinced him that he could make a better job of running the country himself, and he announced that he would run for president. In 1964 a "Dizzy for Pres" button was the world's hippest fashion accessory, but unfortunately this was not enough to get him elected.

His unique musical style continued to evolve long after bebop had receded. As it mellowed, his style revealed quite clearly the elements that linked him to the great jazz trumpet tradition, back through Roy Eldridge and the great swing trumpeters to Louis Armstrong. The immensely long, curling phrases, the fearless pursuit of an idea through remote harmonic territory, the sheer imaginative force burning away behind those ballooning cheeks and owlish glasses were uniquely his own.

It is impossible to overestimate the influence of John Birks Gillespie on the course of jazz, especially jazz trumpet playing. He set the stringent technical standards that young professionals are still expected to meet. Just as important, he kept everyone's spirits up and proved by example that it was possible to play perfectly serious music without being glum.

Dizzy Gillespie solos in front of his big band at New York's Royal Roost Club in 1948, the year when bebop became a brief popular craze. The floppy bow ties, part of the band uniform being worn by saxophonists Ernie Henry and Joe Gayles, were the height of bebop fashion at the time.

Benny Goodman

1 9 0 9 - 1 9 8 6

According to ancient legend, the swing era began on August 21, 1935. That was the night when Benny Goodman and his 14-piece orchestra appeared at the Palomar Ballroom, Los Angeles, and the patrons stopped dancing to crowd around the bandstand and cheer. Goodman was aged 26 at the time and had already been a professional musician for half his life. Born amid great poverty in the Chicago ghetto, he had worked his way through several bands and made innumerable recordings as a sideman before forming his own band. At first he met with little success, but eventually he found his audience—young people born around the end of World War I who became the Swing Generation and who crowned Goodman "King of Swing."

His success was richly deserved. The band made a phenomenally heart-lifting sound, especially when playing music specially tailored for it by the great arranger Fletcher Henderson. And Goodman himself played almost impossibly fluent and limpid clarinet, which was heard at its best in the small groups, "bands within the band," that he introduced in order to add variety to his shows.

The trio, featuring pianist Teddy Wilson, and the quartet, with vibraphonist Lionel Hampton added, caused a sensation on their own account. It was a bold move, in the 1930s, to introduce these two African-American players into an all-white band, but Goodman never backed down for an instant. Later he brought in the great Charlie Christian on guitar and trumpeter Cootie Williams, from Duke Ellington's orchestra. Even when the swing craze had blown itself out, Goodman continued to lead great bands, as well as branching out into classical music. His powers as an instrumentalist just went on increasing, almost to the end.

Benny Goodman was a man of great vision and influence, yet there was something in his makeup that made people dislike and even fear him. His cold, disapproving stare, known as "the ray," was famous among musicians. Generations of ex-Goodman sidemen had tales to tell of his appalling lack of consideration for anyone except himself. Tenor saxophonist Zoot Sims summed it all up on his return from a tour of the Soviet Union with Goodman. "How was it with Benny in Russia?" a reporter asked. "Every gig with Benny's like playing in Russia," replied Zoot.

Nevertheless, Goodman remains the greatest name in jazz clarinet. Clarinettists who followed him had to make a conscious effort to avoid his influence if they were ever to avoid sounding like mere imitations.

Benny Goodman in rehearsal during the late 1940s. By then the "King of Swing" had begun his slow self-transformation into the staid, absent-minded, slightly remote figure of later years.

Dexter Gordon

1 9 2 3 - 1 9 9 0

Dexter Keith Gordon, the six-foot five (1.84 m) giant of the tenor saxophone, had instant star quality. Everything about him matched his physical size. He played with immense deliberation and an air of calm authority, and he knew how to wear a suit better than anyone else in the business. Indeed, he was the only man ever to have lectured Miles Davis on the subject of dress and how to look hip. Like Miles, he was a child of the middle classes; his father was Duke Ellington's doctor.

Like most musicians of his generation, Dexter served his apprenticeship in the big bands, starting at age 17 with Lionel Hampton and finishing four years later with Billy Eckstine's legendary, ground-breaking bebop outfit. From 1945, moving between his native Los Angeles and New York, he gained acceptance as one of the leading bebop tenors. Dexter's tenor duets, or "duels," with his friendly rival, Wardell Gray, were established crowd-pullers. His career suffered in the 1950s when he was removed from the scene by two long prison sentences for drugs offenses. However, in 1960, when he was released for the second time, Dexter's career really took off. He signed with Blue Note Records and began recording a series of albums that remain classics to this day.

Equally important, in September 1962 he accepted a two-week engagement at Ronnie Scott's club in London. The reception was so ecstatic that the two weeks became a month, offers flooded in from Continental clubs, festivals, and concert halls, and Dexter's European sojourn ended up lasting for 15 years. Coming to Europe, Dexter declared, was like being reborn. "Back home, I'm just a saxophone player, but here I'm a saxophonist—an artist!" America, he observed, had forsaken jazz and turned to rock, whereas Europeans valued jazz as an art form and knew about its history and heritage. He lived the life of a hero, first in Paris and later in Copenhagen, learning to speak passable French and Danish in the process.

Dexter returned to the U.S. in 1977, making frequent return trips to Europe and touring further afield. In 1986, almost a quarter of a century after that first two-week booking at Ronnie Scott's, he starred in the film *Round Midnight*, gaining an Oscar nomination for his part as an American jazzman in Paris. His insistence on getting every detail of setting and performance right had a lot to do with the movie's success.

Dexter Gordon in later years, still a potent force in jazz. His unique tenor saxophone style changed very little over the years, but he adapted it skilfully to fit in with new rhythmic and harmonic ideas. His influence was enormous, especially on European players.

Stephane Grappelli

1 9 0 8 - 1 9 9 7

Jazz is an international musical language, and different nations speak it with their own accents. Stephane Grappelli was among the first major artists to appear outside America and, throughout a long life, created jazz replete with Gallic charm and Parisian savoir-faire. His music had the uniquely French quality of being romantic, at times almost sentimental, but never quite becoming emotionally out of control.

He began teaching himself the violin at the age of 10, imitating the fiddlers who played on café terraces. At 13 he was studying at the Paris Conservatoire, and at 15 began earning his living by playing both violin and piano in cinemas and cafés. In 1929 he joined the top French band of showman-band leader Gregor. A few years later, he was playing in a backstage jam session at the Hotel Claridge, where he met the great Gypsy guitarist Django Reinhardt for the first time. Together they formed an all-string band, the Quintette du Hot Club de France, the first non-American jazz ensemble based on no obvious American model. The Quintette's records, made between 1934 and 1939, make brilliant use of the contrast between Grappelli's melting lightness and Reinhardt's urgency.

The outbreak of World War II in 1939 separated the partners. Grappelli spent the war years in London, playing in West End nightclubs and appearing in five British films. Although he returned to France in 1946, Grappelli adopted England as his second home and spent long periods there. However, he took care never to lose his stage-Frenchman's accent, which the British found so charming.

Changing fashions in jazz diverted public attention for a while. In the early 1970s, he was leading a small band at the Paris Hilton when he recorded a sensational album, *Paris Encounter* (1972), with the young American vibraphonist Gary Burton. The entire jazz world was startled by the audacity of his playing. This was the start of Grappelli's remarkable, late-flowering second career.

In 1972 the British guitarist Diz Disley formed a band on the Quintette pattern and invited Grappelli to lead it for a short tour. The results surpassed their wildest dreams, with venues around the world clamoring to book the band. They played the Newport Jazz Festival in 1973 and Carnegie Hall in 1974. The rising curve of Grappelli's creativity continued through his sixties and seventies. In his eighties he was playing better than ever. Only death, shortly before his 90th birthday, could stop him.

Grappelli continued performing at his very best into extreme old age. His early career had been shared with the mercurial Django Reinhardt, whose erratic brilliance had an unsettling effect on Grappelli. On his own, and recognized as a great and original artist, he blossomed.

Musser

Lionel Hampton

b. 1909

Lionel Hampton was the first vibraphone virtuoso. In fact, he introduced the instrument into jazz. He was also a larger-than-life stage performer, leading a series of raucously exciting bands, playing two-fingered piano at breakneck speed, jumping on drums, inciting audiences to acts of joyous disorder. If the management had to call the riot squad before the night was out, Hamp considered he'd done a good job. On the other hand, his work as a serious jazz improviser was a matter of great delicacy and logic. Once embarked upon one of his long solos, often unaccompanied, he became a different person—completely absorbed and oblivious to his surroundings.

Hampton was brought up in Chicago during the 1920s, when the city was the jazz capital of the world and home to the first generation of jazz masters. King Oliver, Louis Armstrong, Bessie Smith, Earl Hines—he heard them all in person at an early and impressionable age. He attended a Catholic school, where he was trained as a drummer by a nun, Sister Petra, and in his early teens joined the newsboys' band sponsored by the *Chicago Defender* newspaper. At 18 Hampton moved to Los Angeles and joined Paul Howard's Quality Serenaders. This was when he met Gladys Neal, who became his wife, manager, and financial controller for the next 42 years. He first played the vibraphone on record at a Louis Armstrong session in 1930.

Hamp's big break came in 1936 when he joined Benny Goodman's band as a featured soloist. Soon he was also recording under his own name for Victor Records. He was allowed to play whatever he liked and use whichever musicians he chose. The results, released as *Lionel Hampton and his Orchestra* (1937–40), add up to 90 numbers featuring the cream of the swing era, playing in relaxed and informal groups. Hampton himself plays vibraphone, drums, piano, and sings.

Leaving Goodman in 1940, he set up the first of his big bands, a wild, roaring affair that anticipated the rhythm and blues style by almost a decade. The band featured a string of tenor saxophone soloists—Illinois Jaquet, Arnett Cobb, Eddie Chamblee—who specialized in frenzied, hysterical solos.

In 1943, Hampton alleges, he discovered a 19-year-old vocalist named Ruth Jones, renamed her Dinah Washington, and launched her career. As time passed, the advancing years obliged him to calm down a little, but he has remained a potent force into extreme old age.

Once settled behind the vibraphone and embarked on one of his long solos, Hampton was lost in the music. This picture from the 1960s catches that side of him exactly. At other times, he could be like a man possessed, shouting encouragement and jumping around the stage.

Herbie Hancock

b. 1940

Herbie Hancock is extravagantly gifted. A child prodigy, he played a Mozart piano concerto with the Chicago Philharmonic at the age of 11. At Grinnell College, Des Moines, he graduated twice, first in electrical engineering and again in music. He composed some of the best-known jazz standards of the past 30 years, including "Watermelon Man," "Cantaloupe Island," and "Dolphin Dance," and he virtually invented the style of music known as "jazz fusion."

The moment he appeared on the New York jazz scene, as a 22-year-old pianist with trumpeter Donald Byrd, Hancock caused a sensation. He was signed by Blue Note Records, and within a year his debut album, *Takin' Off* (1962), had made his name. It also laid the basis of his fortunes because one of the tracks was the original "Watermelon Man," destined to spawn literally dozens of cover versions over the years.

He joined Miles Davis in 1963 and, along with bassist Ron Carter and drummer Tony Williams, created a rhythm section that changed the entire shape of contemporary jazz. This trio stretched the traditional function of the rhythm section almost to breaking point, but, magically, the thread never actually snapped, no matter how far they pulled it. Miles's records of 1963–68—including *My Funny Valentine* (1964), *ESP* (1965), and *The Sorcerer* (1967)—are packed with wonderful moments of rhythmic and harmonic virtuosity by the Hancock-led rhythm section. Neither he nor Miles ever surpassed the music created during those years. Although he was a full-time member of the Miles Davis Quintet, Hancock continued to record for Blue Note under his own name. One of these albums, the magnificent *Maiden Voyage* (1965), rivaled Miles's own in its impact on the worldwide jazz audience.

After leaving Miles in 1968, Hancock concentrated on bringing together jazz and elements of rock and world music. The early 1970s saw a rapid advance in the technology of musical electronics, and Hancock, like Miles, turned increasingly to these resources. He was an early exponent of such instruments as the Fender-Rhodes electric piano, the clavinet, and the first generation of polyphonic synthesizers. His hit album of 1973, *Headhunters*, sounded at times like a demonstration record for the latest technology. This fascination with electronic wizardry has continued ever since, but Hancock remains a supremely accomplished musician, more than able to hold his own in the most advanced conventional jazz company.

Herbie Hancock playing a synthesizer in 1981. During the late 1970s, Hancock achieved considerable success in the commercial pop charts, and gained a reputation for pioneering new kinds of electronic music.

Coleman Hawkins

1904-1969

Although the 1920s are known as the jazz age, and although today the saxophone is the instrument most closely identified with jazz, saxophone playing in the 1920s was dire. Apart from the untypical case of Sidney Bechet's soprano, saxophones in the jazz age produced the kind of damp belch normally associated with bad plumbing. It was not until November 1929 that anyone recorded a real, convincingly musical jazz solo on the tenor saxophone. The tune was "Hello, Lola," the band was the Mound City Blue Blowers, and the player was 25-year-old Coleman Hawkins. His tone was full and sensuous, his technique agile and fluent, and the ideas bold and assured.

Hawkins had virtually invented the tenor saxophone as a serious instrument and, from that moment on, the way he played it was universally accepted as the only way to play. He was the unchallenged star of Fletcher Henderson's great orchestra and in huge demand as a soloist for recording sessions. Then, in 1934, he suddenly announced that he felt like a change of scene, left Henderson, and sailed for Europe. Nowadays this would not raise any eyebrows, but in those days his move made headlines in the musical press. His presence had an incalculable effect on the development of European jazz, as the records he made in Britain, France, and Holland during his five-year stay reveal.

Returning home in 1939, just before the outbreak of World War II, Hawkins discovered that during his absence a challenger to his supremacy had arisen in the form of Lester Young. Assembling a nine-piece band, he took up residence at the New York club Kelly's Stable and signed with Victor Records. At the first Victor session he recorded the ballad "Body and Soul," one of the great jazz classics, as near perfect as a piece of improvised music can be.

Throughout the 1940s, his name was never absent from the neon signs above the most prestigious clubs. When bebop came along, upsetting life for most of his contemporaries, he embraced it eagerly, briefly employing both Dizzy Gillespie and Thelonious Monk.

In the 1950s and early 1960s, he toured as a solo attraction, often with the all-star show Jazz at the Philharmonic. Always keen to keep up to date, he recorded a bossa nova album, *Desafinado*, in 1963. In the end, having achieved so much, he seems to have become bored with life. He virtually gave up eating, drank brandy all day, and died of self-neglect.

Coleman Hawkins in his late 1940s heyday, playing at a 52nd Street club in New York. His tenor saxophone was a gift from the manufacturers, Selmer of Paris. It was coated in a triple layer of gold plate, making it one of the heaviest saxophones in history.

Fletcher Henderson

1 8 9 7 - 1 9 5 2

Benny Goodman may have been the "King of Swing," but swing would not have sounded as exciting as it did without Fletcher Henderson, the architect of the swinging big band. It was Henderson who provided the scores to some of Goodman's most successful numbers—"King Porter Stomp," "When Buddha Smiles," "Christopher Columbus," "Henderson Stomp"—and who led one of the most star-studded black bands of the period.

A mild, unassertive man from a respectable middle-class family, Henderson would have got nowhere at all had he not been in the right place at the right time. His talent was undoubted, but he was shy and passive. He waited for things to happen to him and, fortunately, they were mainly good things.

First, in 1920 he got a part-time job with a music publisher, Pace-Handy, which just happened to specialize in blues songs at the start of a huge blues craze. Then he was sent on tour playing piano for singer Ethel Waters, who turned out to be a star in the making. In 1922 in New Orleans, he heard an unknown young cornet player called Louis Armstrong play. In 1923 he went along with a bunch of musicians for an audition, which they passed. Henderson was promptly nominated as leader on account of his genteel manners.

Armstrong played with the band for several months, his influence starting the process that turned it from an ordinary dance orchestra into an embryo swing band. The band grew around him, the arranger left in 1927, and Fletcher was obliged to take over, discovering his true talent for writing swinging scores almost by accident. As a band leader he was quite hopeless, far too easy-going, but luckily his wife, Leora, was a forceful personality and kept the musicians more or less in order.

And so it went on, the band regularly falling apart and being reformed, losing one top soloist and finding another. Musicians loved playing in it, but it was a precarious life. And then, in 1934, Goodman—virtually broke himself—commissioned Henderson to write some scores for his new band. These were the ones he was playing at the moment of his great breakthrough in August 1935. His gratitude and his admiration for Henderson were boundless. "Each score was a classic," Goodman recalled. "I really thought he was a genius." Fletcher's arrangements and Benny's band-leading made a perfect marriage. They worked together almost until Fletcher's death.

Fletcher Henderson, toward the end of his life, leading a sextet at New York's Café Society. He was a good but not spectacular pianist. Although he never severed his connection with Benny Goodman, Henderson always liked to maintain a degree of independence.

Woody Herman

1913 - 1987

Woody Herman was known as the "Road Father" because for nearly half a century successive generations of young musicians came up through his touring band. Of the three great clarinet-playing leaders—Benny Goodman, Artie Shaw, and Herman—Woody was by far the most open-minded and welcoming to fresh talent. He kept up with new ideas in jazz and often influenced developments. If former members are to be believed, his band was always fun to play with, even in the hardest of times, and the records bear this out.

Woody started in show business at the age of eight, singing and dancing in vaudeville. By the age of 10, billed as "The Boy Wonder," he was also playing clarinet and saxophone. He joined his first band at 17 and became a band leader at 23, taking over the remnants of the successful Isham Jones Orchestra when Jones retired. The first Woody Herman Orchestra bore the subtitle "The Band that Plays the Blues," an unusual choice for a white band at the time, but fully justified by their soulful sound. Their first big hit in 1939, "Woodchopper's Ball," was a 12-bar blues. His subsequent bands, known to posterity as "Herman's Herds," were all intensely swinging affairs, packed with great soloists, many of whom first made their name with Woody.

The First Herd, containing saxophonist Flip Phillips, trombonist Bill Harris, and the trumpet-playing brothers Pete and Conte Candoli, had a phenomenal run of hit records between 1944 and 1946. Among them were "Apple Honey," "Caldonia," and "The Good Earth." The band's vocalist, Frances Wayne, also scored a huge success with "Happiness Is Just a Thing Called Joe."

The Second Herd, from 1947 to 1949, included a saxophone section with three tenor saxophones—Stan Getz, Zoot Sims, and Herbie Steward—and Serge Chaloff on baritone. They became known as the "Four Brothers," after the feature number specially written for them by arranger Jimmy Giuffre.

The Third Herd, the first to tour internationally, ran through the 1950s with a constantly changing personnel of young stars, such as trombonist Urbie Green and tenor saxophonist Phil Urso. Then, in 1962, came the Swinging Herd, a high-energy 17-piece of blistering power, as overwhelming in its way as the First Herd. This was the last identifiable Herd, with later bands growing out of it.

Unlike most other big-band leaders, Woody would have no truck with nostalgia. Even when he played old favorites, they were always given a new twist.

Woody Herman recording with his Second Herd in 1948. The vibraphonist in the foreground is 23-year-old Terry Gibbs. Like all Herman's bands, this one contained a judicious mixture of youth and experience. Among other youthful members were saxophonists Stan Getz and Zoot Sims.

Earl Hines

Father _(handwritten, inserted before Hines)_

1 9 0 3 - 1 9 8 3

Count Basie once remarked, "If you run up against Earl, you're likely to get bruised." A lot of pianists learned this the hard way, taking turns with Earl Hines at jam sessions. He possessed a musical mind of endless subtlety, a dazzling technique, and the competitive instincts of a champion boxer. In his youth, Hines was the man who finally liberated jazz piano from the apron strings of ragtime. As he grew older, he went on getting better, so that in his seventies he was still one of the half-dozen finest jazz pianists on earth.

He first came to the notice of jazz lovers in 1928, playing a duet with Louis Armstrong entitled "Weather Bird." It was the first time, apart from an early tangle with Sidney Bechet, that Armstrong had encountered another musician who was more or less his equal, and the combination of the two is quite awesome. One technique invented by Hines is the practice of playing the melody in octaves, with a little tremolo on the final note of each phrase, like a trumpet player's vibrato. It is such an effective way of personalizing a melodic line that pianists are still using it today. Nat "King" Cole, one of Hines's most talented disciples, employed "trumpet-style" octaves regularly.

Hines was an extrovert character, a natural leader. He led a series of excellent big bands during the swing era and was resident for many years at Chicago's Grand Terrace Ballroom. Like Woody Herman, he had a great ear for new talent and was no lover of convention. As early as 1942 he recognized the potential of struggling young bebop players such as Dizzy Gillespie. At one time his band contained both Dizzy and Charlie Parker, and his vocalist was Billy Eckstine. Looking for someone to take over the piano stool occasionally, while he chatted to the customers, he hired a shy young woman named Sarah Vaughan for the job. He soon persuaded her to add singing to her job description. Everyone who knew Hines referred to him as "Fatha," a recognition of his role as father-figure in so many lives.

Apart from a spell with Louis Armstrong's All-Stars from 1948 to 1951, Fatha was always his own boss. He found it difficult to play a subordinate role to anyone, even Louis, and it was a relief to them both when Earl left. Honors were deservedly heaped upon him in his later years—recitals at the White House, audiences with the pope—and he kept playing until the day before his death, then aged 79.

The cigar was a stage prop, part of his image, along with the tilted hat. Earl Hines was always very conscious of his presentation and appearance. In later years, he wore an extraordinary wig, which looked as though it was made out of textured toffee.

Billie Holiday

1 9 1 5 - 1 9 5 9

A tall bar stool, an old-fashioned microphone, an upright piano with a half-full bottle of gin on top of it. The lights dim, the piano tinkles an introduction, and the ritual tale begins. In fringe theaters, studio workshops, and arts festivals around the world (not to mention books, magazines, and one truly appalling film), Billie's story is always the same—one of drugs, drink, racism, violence, jail, and self-destruction.

Poor Billie! What drives people to continue heaping these indignities upon her, decades after her death? Could it just be an arty form of the voyeurism that drew audiences in her last few years on earth, waiting for her to fall over or get arrested? Or is it that, as one writer put it, feeling bad about Billie makes people feel good about themselves? Whatever the case, the final impression is always the same: that Billie is special because of the horrible things that happened to her. This is a dreadful insult. Horrible things happen to people all the time, but there was only one Billie Holiday.

She is special because she could take a simple song, such as "Back in Your Own Backyard," lift it gently out of its song-copy straitjacket, and set it swinging so blithely that you just have to smile. She could sing a line such as "I've met so many men with fascinating ways," and conjure from it a whole lifetime of experience. Her musicianship was awesome. John Hammond, the record producer who discovered her singing in a Harlem dive early in 1933, recalled: "The way she sang around a melody, her uncanny harmonic sense, were almost unbelievable in a girl of 17."

Musicians were the first to appreciate her qualities and to understand that here was something unique in singing. It wasn't blues or musical comedy or even popular music in the usual sense of the term. It was pure jazz. Her phrasing had a severe elegance that recalled Louis Armstrong and the airy lightness of Lester Young, her dearest friend.

As time passed, and her life became darkened by drugs, predatory men, and other misfortunes, her singing lost its pristine lightness of earlier years. She chose songs that cast her in the role of victim, and even wrote some herself, such as "God Bless the Child" and "Don't Explain." But what was lost in exuberant invention was replaced by an unblinking honesty of delivery. That is why Billie Holiday is special.

A publicity shot from the mid-1940s, featuring Billie's ever-present gardenia. She first wore one to cover a patch of hair burned by curling tongs. This photograph was taken during her early years as a solo star, contracted to Decca Records. She was the first black singer to record a ballad with string orchestra accompaniment.

Abdullah Ibrahim

b. 1934

In the 1950s, a generation of jazz musicians arose in South Africa. They began by emulating the American players they heard on records, but gradually forged a unique style that owed much to their African heritage. Among them was a young pianist named Dollar Brand, a devotee of Duke Ellington with ambitions to compose and lead a band.

After serving his apprenticeship with outfits bearing such splendid names as the Streamline Brothers and the Tuxedo Slickers, in 1960 he formed the Jazz Epistles, which became the first African jazz group to release a whole album—*Jazz Epistles: Verse I* (1960). In the same year the Sharpeville massacre occurred, and in its wake, both resistance to apartheid and the oppression of black Africans increased dramatically. By 1962 it had become virtually impossible for African musicians to function under the restrictions of apartheid, and Brand, along with his future wife, the singer Bea Benjamin, left for Europe and settled in Zurich.

The following year, while on a European tour, Duke Ellington heard them. He was so impressed that he financed a recording session and recommended Brand to important bookers and agents. By 1965 Brand was working in New York, collaborating with John Coltrane, Ornette Coleman, and Don Cherry on experiments with free-form jazz.

In 1968 he converted to Islam, taking the name Abdullah Ibrahim (Bea Benjamin took the name Sathima), and returned to Africa. There he began developing his highly personal variant of African jazz, featuring ethnic instruments, ritual chants, dance rhythms, and the harmonies of African choral singing. He was now an artist with an international reputation, able to travel freely between South Africa, Europe, and America.

But all South African artists were committed to the freedom struggle, and when Ibrahim organized a jazz festival in 1976, deliberately ignoring the rules on strict separation of the races, he was forced to leave the country. He did not return until the fall of the apartheid regime and the election of Nelson Mandela as president of South Africa in 1994.

In 1982 his hugely ambitious multimedia work *Kalahari Liberation* was produced at a number of European festivals to great critical acclaim. Much of his later music has been created for his seven-piece band Ekaya, formed in 1983. The story of Ibrahim's phenomenal growth as an artist is told by records made over 40 years, and he continues to inspire new generations of African jazz musicians.

Abdullah Ibrahim continues to record and play concerts as a solo artist. He is able to establish a close rapport with audiences around the world through the power of his music alone.

Milt Jackson

1923 - 1999

For reasons lost in the mists of time, Milt Jackson was known to one and all as "Bags," which accounts for the title of his best-known composition, the 12-bar blues "Bags' Groove." Bags was the greatest vibraphone player of his generation and a huge influence on all who followed him. Although his solos are packed with notes, they are always surprisingly easy to follow because the outlines are so clear. It seems impossible that such long, rippling streams of notes could be produced by a single pair of mallets.

Milt's tone is unmistakable, too—sharp and clear, but occasionally warmed by a lazy, sensuous vibrato. He was the first vibraphonist to work seriously on the mechanics of tone and to investigate what could be created musically by tinkering with the instrument's vibrator fans, turning them off and on and adjusting their speed.

Dizzy Gillespie came across Milt in 1945, playing in a local Detroit band, and took him under his wing. He was featured with Dizzy's first big band, formed in 1946, although the rather crude instrument he had at the time did not show him at his best. However, in 1948 he recorded a session with Thelonious Monk and his playing, especially on the classic "Misterioso," came as a revelation.

Meanwhile, Gillespie's pianist, John Lewis, was working on compositions for a jazz "chamber quartet." In 1951, along with bassist Ray Brown and drummer Kenny Clarke, they made their first recordings together as the Milt Jackson Quartet. By 1952 they had become the Modern Jazz Quartet, with Percy Heath replacing Brown on bass. Lewis, a classically trained musician, set the tone of the MJQ from the start, producing elegantly charming pieces in semi-classical form, with titles such as "The Queen's Fancy," "The Golden Striker," and "Fontessa." These did not give much scope for the long, swinging solos that were Jackson's forte, but they displayed his beauty of tone and delicacy of touch to perfection. And at every concert there came the moment when Bags was let loose to spread himself. Thus the balance between formality and improvisation was maintained, and the MJQ enjoyed an uninterrupted run of 22 successful years.

Away from the Quartet, Jackson recorded on equal terms with some of the greatest names in jazz. Among these albums were *Soul Brothers* (1957) with Ray Charles, *Plenty, Plenty Soul* (1957) with Cannonball Adderley, *Bags & Trane* (1959) with John Coltrane, and *Two of the Few* (1983), a phenomenal duet session with Oscar Peterson.

Milt Jackson, pictured in the late 1940s, playing with Dizzy Gillespie's big band. The smiling bass player behind his right shoulder is a young Ray Brown, who became part of the Milt Jackson Quartet in 1951.

Keith Jarrett

b. 1945

Jarrett has been described as "the most influential living pianist," not just in jazz but in contemporary music as a whole. As if this were not enough, his recordings of Bach's "The Well-Tempered Clavier" (playing harpsichord) and several Mozart piano concertos have met with great critical acclaim.

In fact, you could say that Keith Jarrett is the complete musician. He began playing the piano at three and gave his first full-length recital at the age of seven. Becoming interested in jazz as a teenager, he studied at Berklee College of Music, Boston, and was a member of Art Blakey's Jazz Messengers at 20. But it was with saxophonist Charles Lloyd's quartet that he really made his mark. He joined Lloyd in 1966, which was very good timing because this was the exact moment when many of the musical conventions of jazz were beginning to break down, offering great scope for original and adventurous musicians. The presence of Jarrett and the innovative drummer Jack DeJohnette ensured the success of Lloyd's band, and it toured the world many times during Jarrett's three years.

Leaving Lloyd in 1969, he led his own trio for a while before joining Miles Davis in 1970. Once again, his timing was good because this was the exact moment when Miles made one of his great leaps into a new and unexplored genre—in this case, jazz-rock. The move brought Jarrett a whole new audience and also enlarged his reputation.

But the most important association of his career came in 1971, when he joined German producer Manfred Eicher's ECM label and recorded the first of his astonishing solo albums, *Facing You* (1971). From this point, Jarrett's solo recitals grew to become unique phenomena in the world of music. He would play non-stop for up to two hours, improvising absolutely from scratch, creating endless kaleidoscopic pictures in harmony, melody, and rhythm. Recordings of these marathons scored huge sales, especially the 1975 double album *The Köln Concert*. The question of whether or not this music falls within the definition of jazz, although sometimes asked, is irrelevant. It is, in Duke Ellington's phrase, "beyond category," but it would not have existed in this form if jazz itself had not already been in existence.

The list of Keith Jarrett's recordings is immensely long and includes collaborations with many of the greatest names in contemporary music, and there is not a single lazy or ill-considered note in any one of them.

Keith Jarrett is one of the most admired musicians of the modern era, regardless of genre. His talents extend far beyond jazz. Not only has he written and performed works for piano and symphony orchestra, but his recording of J.S. Bach's harpsichord suite "The Well-Tempered Clavier" is also regarded as among the finest modern versions of the work.

Bunk Johnson

1 8 8 9 - 1 9 4 9

It's an extraordinary tale. The story of the resurrection and virtual canonization of William Geary Johnson is part heroic saga and part romantic fantasy, enlivened by a dash of farce. It goes like this.

In 1939, at the height of the swing era, an interest in early styles of jazz was just beginning to stir among a few enthusiasts. What did those first New Orleans pioneers really sound like? Jazz had been developing and changing at such a pace that, in the absence of recordings, there was not much to go on. But jazz was then only about 40 years old, the same age as Louis Armstrong. Who did Armstrong remember hearing as a boy? "Well," said Louis, "there was Buddy Bolden and King Oliver and Buddy Petit, and there was old Bunk Johnson, too. He could play real good." Bolden, Oliver, and Petit were dead, but might the legendary Bunk Johnson still be alive?

Extensive inquiries by two young fans, Frederick Ramsey and William Russell, revealed only that he had last been heard of driving a truck in the rice fields around New Iberia, Louisiana. To their astonishment, a letter addressed to him, care of the New Iberia postmaster, elicited a reply from Bunk himself. He had not played for years, he wrote. He was broke and had lost all his teeth.

Excited by their discovery, Ramsey and Russell sent money and a new trumpet, and arranged for Sidney Bechet's dentist brother, Leonard, to make Bunk a set of dentures. In 1942 in a room above a New Orleans music shop, Bunk, accompanied by a specially assembled band, made his first recordings. It would be pulling punches to say that the results were a bit rough. By all normal standards, they were dire.

Nevertheless, the whole project caught the imagination of the jazz world and created great excitement. Opinion was divided, and for the first time in jazz, huge aesthetic questions were broached. Is the concept of "progress" applicable to any form of art? How important is authenticity? If simple music sounds naive, is that because the ear is corrupted by sophistication?

With the passage of time, Bunk regained some of his former skill, and it was possible to get some inkling of the way he must have sounded in his youth—a clear, forceful trumpet lead. The entire New Orleans revival was founded on his example. Planted in the fertile soil of romantic legend, the revival flourished, spreading Bunk's fame across the world. He was a jazz icon, if ever there was one.

Bunk Johnson pictured in his late-flowering prime. He was by no means the kindly and easy-going old gentleman of legend. He was only in his fifties when he was rediscovered, and had decided views of his own about the way his career should be managed.

J.J. Johnson

b. 1924

The trombone, with its unwieldy slide, is not ideally suited to the rapid, angular lines of bebop. J.J. Johnson was the first trombonist to show that bebop was even possible on the instrument when he played with Charlie Parker and Dizzy Gillespie in the late 1940s.

All technical progress has its losses as well as its gains, and in achieving his prodigious speed and agility, Johnson was obliged to sacrifice most of the traditional trombone vocabulary. Out went the smears, whoops, slides, and bizarre muted effects that contribute so much charm to earlier styles of jazz, to be replaced by a bright, even, hard-edged tone, rather like a big trumpet. In fact, people hearing Johnson for the first time often thought that he was playing a valve-trombone, although he never did.

Despite this notable achievement, Johnson found work quite scarce in those early days. He recorded with Miles Davis's Birth of the Cool band in 1949, but was reduced, in the early 1950s, to taking a daytime job and playing part-time. Then, in 1954, he teamed up with his closest rival, the Danish-born trombonist Kai Winding. As Jay & Kai they quickly became one of the big attractions on the growing jazz concert and club circuit. Their tones blended beautifully and a repertoire of tuneful, witty arrangements assured their popularity. One piece in particular, the scampering "Don't Argue," in which the trombones chased one another like a pair of hyperactive kittens, always brought the house down.

Johnson was becoming more and more interested in writing music, first for records under his own name. Then he began producing background scores for television, and as his reputation grew, moved to Hollywood to concentrate on writing. Fortunately, he still kept his trombone technique in shape. He was friendly with André Previn, and together they made a delightful album devoted to the music of Kurt Weill, featuring Johnson's trombone—*André Previn and J.J. Johnson Play Mack the Knife and Bilbao Song* (1961). It was an interesting meeting of minds: Previn, the classical musician who took to jazz, and Johnson, a leading jazz musician moving in the opposite direction.

In later years Johnson re-emerged as a player, mellower and less concerned to demonstrate his technique all the time. With this new, relaxed attitude, his tone blossomed into a warm, golden glow. In 1994 Johnson recorded what many consider his masterpiece, a CD entitled *Tangence*, accompanied by a full, 50-piece concert orchestra, arranged and conducted by his hero, Robert Farnon.

J.J. Johnson at a Blue Note recording session in 1953. His mercurial technique showed that the trombone was capable of handling the fast-moving lines of bebop.

Elvin Jones

b. 1927

Elvin is the youngest of the three famous Jones brothers, the other two being pianist Hank and trumpeter Thad. It is impossible to believe that the great John Coltrane Quartet of the early 1960s could have reached the heights it did without the surging energy of Elvin Jones's drums pushing it along. His sound, like Atlantic rollers—shifting, tumbling, but somehow inevitable—embodied Coltrane's whole approach. The interaction between them was so intense that the drums were sometimes clearly dictating the course of the performance, not merely providing rhythmic accompaniment.

Elvin looks so relaxed when he is playing that he seems to be moving in slow motion, but his constructions are full of surprise and wit. Watching him can be slightly disconcerting because nothing seems to happen in a regular pattern. With most other drummers, the hi-hat cymbals snap together on the second and fourth beats of each bar, the right hand plays a steady pattern on the top cymbal, and so on. In Elvin's case, the whole process appears quite random, yet out of it comes this irresistible, rolling pulse that is all his own.

Since the Coltrane Quartet days, Elvin has led a series of bands, organized rather on the Art Blakey pattern of constant renewal and a steady throughput of new, young talent. Saxophonists Dave Liebman, Pat LaBarbera, and the late Joe Farrell all enhanced their careers by spells with Elvin Jones.

Most drumming band leaders tend to assert their position by playing at deafening volume all the time, but Elvin relies on subtlety rather than muscle. For all that, he is a powerfully built man who, even into his seventies, looks dauntingly fit.

Before each performance, his diminutive Japanese wife, Keiko, comes on stage and tunes the drum kit, a job that few serious percussionists delegate to anyone. Keiko's touch in setting up the kit obviously plays a part in the remarkable clarity and definition of Elvin's sound. This clarity is essential, because the rhythmic patterns often become so complex that a muddy sound would make them quite incomprehensible.

Elvin Jones is one of the great innovators of jazz drumming, along with Jo Jones, Max Roach, and Tony Williams. His influence reaches beyond jazz and into contemporary music of many kinds. He has set phenomenally high standards of sheer technique, and uncovered vast possibilities in multi-layered rhythms that will provide inspiration to generations of percussionists.

Elvin Jones expanded the horizons of all jazz percussion through his work with the John Coltrane Quartet. His influence extends into free jazz, but Elvin's own playing has always been distinguished for its rolling, pulsing beat.

Jo Jones

Modern jazz drumming starts with Jo Jones. Until he came along, drummers played the beat on the snare and bass drums. However delicately or subtly it was done, this approach still betrayed the instrument's origins in military and marching bands. Jo shifted the job of stating the beat to the hi-hat cymbals, instantly changing the whole perspective of the jazz rhythm section.

The hi-hat consists of two cymbals, mounted face-to-face, one attached to a rod operated by the drummer's left foot. The foot comes down and the cymbals clash together. Jo created his rhythms by beating the hi-hat with a stick, at the same time half-opening and closing it to create varying densities. It sounds complicated in words, but gloriously simple in musical reality.

This was the beat that powered the matchless rhythm section of Count Basie's first band, the finest of the entire swing era. Jo knew perfectly well how superior Basie's section was and, never a man given to false modesty, often said so: "Fletcher Henderson? McKinney's Cotton Pickers? They never had a rhythm section. Chick Webb? Great, but never had a rhythm section. What other rhythm section? None!" Certainly, every important development in jazz drumming since then has used cymbals as the primary timekeeper.

Jo Jones began performing at a very early age. "I was always a gypsy, and had an unusual urge to be in carnivals and circuses," he recalled. Experience, he maintained, was the only reliable teacher, and he brought all his accumulated knowhow, gained originally as a dancer and entertainer in traveling shows, to the business of jazz drumming.

Basie's rhythm section attained its unequaled smoothness and drive in the same way that a great circus troupe perfects its act—by constant practice. Together, the four of them developed a unique, subdued pulse. The original Basie rhythm section stuck together for eight euphoric years, bassist Walter Page leaving in 1942 and Jones being drafted into the army in 1944. The team was reunited for another two-year spell in 1946.

Jo never joined another band permanently after that. Instead, he lived the freelance life around New York, recording many albums throughout the 1950s, 1960s, and 1970s, often with players of his own generation, such as Lester Young and Roy Eldridge. His friend and record producer John Hammond remarked around this time: "I think Jo can do more things superlatively well than any drummer I have ever heard."

Always dapper and immaculate, Jo Jones believed in the traditional values of show business, but nothing was allowed to interfere with the serious job of producing driving, uncluttered swing.

Louis Jordan

1 9 0 8 - 1 9 7 5

There are singers whose voices can conjure the soft romance of a June night or the dewy freshness of a May morning. But when it comes to food, drink, cheerful lechery, and explaining the events of the night before to the judge on the morning after, there's only one choice, and it's the irrepressible Louis Jordan. No song ever summed up a popular entertainer's appeal better than one of his biggest hits, "Let the Good Times Roll."

Louis was destined by birth and upbringing to make people happy. His father was a musician, a clarinet player with the celebrated Rabbit's Foot Minstrels, and from the age of 12, young Louis would spend his school vacations traveling with him as his apprentice. In time Louis became a very good saxophone player, good enough to earn his living with the instrument through the lean years of the Depression.

He ended up in the ranks of Chick Webb's band, resident at the Savoy Ballroom, the most famous dance hall in the whole of black America. But his background had given him the instincts of an old-time showman, and he could never be really happy until he was the center of attention. It was only a matter of time before he had his own band, which, for reasons too obscure to go into, he called his Tympany Five.

A matter of weeks after the band's launch in 1941, the Japanese bombed Pearl Harbor and the U.S. entered World War II. Soon American forces were spread out across the globe, and Louis Jordan had found his audience—the enlisted ranks, the G.I. Joes, the unwilling warriors. His showman's instinct led him right to them, and they took at once to the shuffling, unmilitary beat of the Tympany Five. Numbers such as "The G.I. Jive," "Choo Choo Ch'Boogie," and "Five Guys Named Moe" went down so well that the war itself might have been laid on purely for Louis' benefit. He had 19 hit records in five years.

In the 1950s, Louis' fortunes declined. Despite his track record, Decca refused to renew his contract and, adding insult to injury, signed up the insipid Bill Haley instead. But from beyond the grave, Louis Jordan had the last laugh. In 1990 the show *Five Guys Named Moe*, based on his music, was the hit of the London season, going on to storm Broadway. It ran for five years. At the end of the 1990s, a craze for the jump and jive music of half a century before was filling the clubs in major cities. Louis Jordan's good-time spirit was abroad yet again.

Put down that racing form and listen to me! Louis Jordan in typical telling-it-like-it-is pose in the late 1940s, at the height of his career. When he was performing, Jordan always established eye contact with members of the audience and addressed them directly.

Stan Kenton

1 9 1 1 - 1 9 7 9

Like extinct species of animals, the big bands died out largely because their habitat shrank until it was too small to sustain them. This habitat was the dance hall. Stan Kenton formed his first band in 1941, which was quite late in the day, but it survived by finding an alternative habitat—namely, the concert hall.

Even in its early days, when it was still essentially a dance band, Kenton's orchestra sounded different. It was louder and brasher than the others, and Kenton cultivated a studiously avant-garde air, intended to convey the impression that his music was a cut above the stuff produced by others. The arrangements were spiced with some mild dissonance, and the very titles of Kenton's most characteristic numbers—"Artistry in Rhythm," "Opus in Pastels," "Collaboration, Lament"—reinforced the notion that here was something bracing and challenging, a new kind of big-band music.

The strategy proved highly successful, and from 1945 onward, Kenton's name was rarely absent from the jazz polls. To be fair, by no means all his music at this period suffered from this pretentiousness. The cheerful bebop of "How High the Moon," featuring June Christy's exuberant scat vocal, remains a delight to this day, and Kenton built up a cast of excellent soloists, including alto saxophonist Art Pepper, trombonist Milt Bernhardt, and drummer Shelly Manne.

In 1949 Kenton folded this band and launched his 43-piece Innovations in Modern Music Orchestra, complete with strings, extra brass and woodwind, and a battery of percussion. Special music was written for this ensemble, most notably Bob Graettinger's full-length work *City Of Glass* (1951). This extraordinary work was the furthest extent of Kenton's exploration beyond the bounds of conventional big-band jazz.

The Innovations Orchestra lasted for a couple of years, but proved too costly to keep going. From 1952 onward, Kenton led a succession of bands, some incorporating experimental elements, such as the mellophonium quartet included in the band of the early 1960s. The quality of the music was often high, thanks to a series of superb arrangers (Gerry Mulligan, Shorty Rogers, Neal Hefti) and soloists (Lee Konitz, Pepper Adams, Laurindo Almeida).

Kenton's most lasting contribution to jazz has probably been in education: his "clinics," established at several U.S. colleges, laid the foundation for the network of jazz courses and "stage bands" now flourishing. Scores published by his Creative World Music form the basis of many a student band's repertoire.

Stan Kenton in 1950 during the lifetime of the gargantuan Innovations in Modern Music Orchestra. His desire to be taken seriously often made him seem pompous and aloof.

Rahsaan Roland Kirk

1 9 3 6 - 1 9 7 7

One of the most remarkable figures in the whole history of jazz, Roland Kirk (he added "Rahsaan" later) was more than just an extraordinary musician—he was a human phenomenon. He could, and regularly did, play three instruments at once. He did this not as a novelty act or a stunt to impress the crowd, but as a perfectly serious way of making music.

Commentators have suggested that, being blind, he couldn't see how impossible it looked. His mere arrival on stage, festooned with instruments, was quite alarming. On straps around his neck were three saxophones with a flute planted in the bell of one of them. Also attached to his person were a siren whistle and a nose flute. He often carried a clarinet, too. For some years, he also brought with him a bag of plastic toy flutes, which he would pass out to the audience, instructing them to join in at certain points.

Nor was this the end of Kirk's inventiveness. One of his saxophones was an ordinary tenor model, but the other two were redesigned to his specifications from long-extinct varieties. One, which he called the "manzello," started life in the 1920s as a saxello, a curved soprano saxophone. The other, the "stritch," was originally a straightened-out alto.

A Roland Kirk performance was an unforgettable experience, and no two sets were ever quite the same. He would roar through an opening riff on the three saxes, let go of two, and produce a blistering solo on the remaining one, topped off with a blast on the siren. Then, as the pianist or bassist took a solo, he might rummage about in his armory, produce the flute, and launch another of his specialties, a voiced flute solo—playing and singing at the same time—rising to a gibbering, hysterical climax.

One of his many other accomplishments was a mastery of circular breathing, the technique of blowing out air while, at the same time, breathing in. This enabled him to play for minutes on end without pausing for breath. And so it would go on for an astonishing hour or more.

And then, at the age of 39, he suffered a stroke that paralyzed his right side. He redesigned the tenor saxophone keywork, devised and mastered a whole new technique, and went back on the road for the final year of his life. As a demonstration of sheer courage and willpower, this must rank with Beethoven working on through his deafness. There has never been anyone like him in jazz.

Rahsaan Roland Kirk in full flight. The instruments are (left to right) flute, manzello, stritch, and tenor saxophone. Also visible, between the stritch and the tenor, is a horn-shaped siren whistle. The sheer weight of all this metal, hanging from his neck on leather straps, must have been immense.

Gene Krupa

1 9 0 9 - 1 9 7 3

The classic big band of the swing era was arranged like a scene in a Hollywood musical of the same period. The ranks of players were set up in a pyramid formation—saxes along the front, trombones and rhythm section behind and above, with the trumpets above them, and, right at the pinnacle, the drummer. What a gift to a natural showman like Gene Krupa! From the moment he joined Benny Goodman's band in late 1934, Krupa was one of its main attractions and an important factor in Goodman's early success.

When he went into the tom-tom routine in his big feature number, "Sing, Sing, Sing," Krupa became like a man possessed. His hair would fly about, his eyes took on a manic stare, his jaws chomped wildly on a wad of gum, arms and legs flailed in all directions. When it was over, the drummer would collapse across his white pearl kit, apparently in the final stages of exhaustion. To the parents of middle America, this image of Gene Krupa in full orgiastic abandon summed up everything they did not want their children to admire. To the teenagers themselves, he was glamor personified.

Krupa left Goodman in 1938 to form his own successful band. One of its features was a number in which all the musicians played drums to create an interlocking maze of exciting cross-rhythms. The band also appeared in several movies, starting in 1941 with *Ball of Fire*, starring Barbara Stanwyck.

The band was well established as a top attraction by 1943, when Krupa was arrested on marijuana charges and for employing an underage band boy. Because of his public image, the case attracted much attention and occasioned expressions of moral outrage in the press. He could have gone to jail for five years, but most of the charges were dismissed on appeal and he was out in less than three months. However, with its leader under arrest and unable to travel, the band had folded, and Krupa went to work again as a sideman, first with Goodman and then with Tommy Dorsey.

He formed a second big band in 1944, featuring, among others, the young Gerry Mulligan, and kept it going until 1951, when he joined the Jazz at the Philharmonic team, leading a trio. In 1954 he teamed up with another great drummer, Cozy Cole, to set up a school of percussion. Although he still played quite regularly, most of his efforts in later years went into studying and teaching percussion. In 1959 a Hollywood film was made of his life. Entitled *Drum Crazy: The Gene Krupa Story*, it featured Sal Mineo in the title role.

This is the image that Gene Krupa diligently promoted—the wild, abandoned drummer, beating up a storm. It made him a highly paid star, and ensured that his career lasted longer than those of many of his contemporaries.

Machito

1912 - 1984

Machito ("The Little Guy") was the nickname of Frank Grillo, which was in turn the semi-Americanized version of Francisco Guitierrez, the figurehead of Afro-Cuban music for four decades. He was born in Tampa, Florida, brought up in Havana, Cuba, and spent much of his early life shuttling between the two, earning a reputation as a *sonero* (lead vocalist) and player of the maracas. In 1937 he came to New York at the invitation of his brother-in-law, Mario Bauzá, who was then playing trumpet with Chick Webb at the Savoy Ballroom. Machito found work with Alberto Iznaga's rumba band, while Bauzá became musical director of Cab Calloway's orchestra.

In 1940 Machito formed his own band and Bauzá joined him the following year. Machito acted as the charismatic front man, while Bauzá supplied the musical expertise. With 10 years' experience in top New York bands, Bauzá had a clear vision of how the power of a big swing band could be wedded to the beguiling rhythms and open-ended forms of Cuban dance music. By dint of some ruthless hiring and firing, he created a sound that had never been heard before and that, for sheer drive and excitement, soon proved quite irresistible.

In 1943, although Machito himself was away on war service at the time, his orchestra had its first hit record with Bauzá's composition "Tanga." In the euphoric atmosphere of the postwar years, this hybrid music, now called "Afro-Cuban," really took off. Not only did it suit the festive mood of the times, it also appealed to musicians looking for new ideas to explore. One of the first to experiment with this new music was Dizzy Gillespie. Bauzá had given him his first big break by hiring him for Calloway's trumpet section in 1939.

By 1948 Afro-Cuban music had become established as a regular ingredient in the jazz of the time, with Machito's name always to the fore. In January of that year, his band shared the stage at Carnegie Hall with Stan Kenton, and its transformation from a Latin-American dance band into an Afro-Cuban jazz orchestra was confirmed. Jazz stars regularly appeared as featured soloists, including Charlie Parker, Dexter Gordon, Flip Phillips, and Howard McGhee. So prevalent did this practice become that a new term, "Cubop," was coined to denote the fusion of Cuban music and bebop.

Machito's orchestra pioneered the marriage of jazz and Latin-American music. Without Machito and Bauzá, the combination would probably never have proved as dynamic or as long-lived as it has.

The rhythm section of Machito's orchestra in 1946 (clockwise): vocalist Graciela (claves), Luis Miranda (conga), René Hernandez (piano), Ubaldo Nieto (timbales), Roberto Rodriguez (bass), Machito (maracas), and José Mangual (bongos).

John McLaughlin

b. 1942

John McLaughlin is one of those rare musicians whose playing is rooted in jazz but which extends far beyond its conventional boundaries. He began playing guitar at age 11, trying to emulate acoustic blues artists such as Big Bill Broonzy, and discovered jazz guitar soon afterward. On the London jazz-blues scene of the 1960s, McLaughlin moved from band to band, broadening his experience and earning a formidable reputation. His 1969 album *Extrapolation*, described as one of the classic albums of the decade, marked the close of his formative London period. He left for the U.S. later that year to join Tony Williams's band, Lifetime, and to work on two seminal Miles Davis albums released in 1969, *In a Silent Way* and *Bitches Brew*.

McLaughlin began taking an interest in Eastern religions during his London days and this deepened with time. When he launched his own band in 1971, he gave it the name the Mahavishnu Orchestra—"Mahavishnu" meaning "divine compassion, power, and justice." The Orchestra scored instant success with its first album, *The Inner Mounting Flame* (1971), even though it was startlingly original and unlike anything tried before in the jazz-rock idiom. All five members of Mahavishnu were virtuoso players, but they worked selflessly to create an ensemble music, rather than a vehicle for a parade of star solos. A second Mahavishnu Orchestra, with French violinist Jean-Luc Ponty included, toured in 1974–75.

In contrast to the electric sounds of Mahavishnu, McLaughlin's next band was an entirely acoustic affair. His involvement with Eastern philosophy had led him to study Indian music, and he now assembled Shakti (meaning "creative intelligence, beauty, and power"), a group of leading Indian musicians, including the great violinist Lakshminarayana Shankar. Once again, despite the unfamiliarity of its music, Shakti was an immediate hit with audiences.

This alternation between electric and acoustic music has been the pattern of McLaughlin's career. Shakti was followed by a further Mahavishnu, and after this came a period when he toured and recorded with the great Spanish guitarist Paco De Lucia. The 1980s saw him featured on Miles Davis's funky album *You're Under Arrest* in 1984 and performing his own Guitar Concerto with the Los Angeles Philharmonic in 1985.

McLaughlin's output in recent years has been as varied as ever. A particularly beautiful piece of work was *Time Remembered* (1993), his interpretations of compositions by pianist Bill Evans with an acoustic guitar quartet.

McLaughlin, a scrupulous perfectionist with an adventurous streak, always puts the music first. He is constantly seeking out new ideas and fresh challenges, and has mastered many techniques and musical idioms.

Wynton Marsalis

b . 1 9 6 1

There have been great trumpet players before, but never one capable of winning simultaneous Grammy Awards in both jazz and classical categories. Wynton Marsalis did it at the age of 22. He is a master of the instrument, a staggeringly accomplished improviser, and a jazz composer of genuine stature. In addition, he has carved out a unique position as a kind of philosopher-king to the jazz world, celebrating the long tradition of the music and developing his own work through study of his great predecessors.

Born the son of a jazz musician, pianist Ellis Marsalis, in New Orleans, he feels a responsibility for maintaining these links. Had it not been for his father, he maintains, he might never have discovered jazz at all. It is so easy for the very concept of jazz as a coherent expressive language to be ignored in favor of the easy option of jazz as a fashion accessory. It is a demanding craft and it has to be learned. "You must learn the language of jazz, which includes the language of the blues, like you would learn a foreign language—by imitation and repetition. The more you do it, the more fluent you get," he says.

This is at the heart of Wynton's educational strategy as artistic director of the jazz program at New York's Lincoln Center. "The long-term goal is to include jazz as an important part of everyone's artistic education—as part of democracy, if you like." He also presides over a repertory company of about 20 top professional musicians capable of tackling anything in the jazz idiom, from Jelly Roll Morton down to the present day.

The major influence on his own work is Duke Ellington. This is particularly evident in long, ambitious works such as *In This House, On This Morning* (1994), a suite cast in the form of a southern Baptist service, the historical oratorio *Blood on the Fields* (1997), and *Big Train* (1999), a musical journey with philosophical overtones. Despite the weighty ideas they are intended to embody, all these pieces burst with energy and good humor. Nothing could be farther from the chilly gloom normally associated with "serious" contemporary jazz composition, partly because there is so much about Wynton's music that is familiar. "Being modern does not mean searching for novelty," he says. "Swing and individual tone and the majesty of the blues are fundamentals that never go out of date."

Marsalis rarely plays classical music nowadays. The techniques are so different, he says, that changing from one to the other is a long and difficult process.

Wynton Marsalis and the curious-looking hand-built trumpet that attracts so much attention from musicians wherever he plays. Designed and built by brass-instrument guru Dave Monette, it has an integral mouthpiece. Other players of Monette trumpets include Terence Blanchard and Guy Barker.

Pat Metheny

b . 1 9 5 4

There is an open, spacious quality about Pat Metheny's music that almost certainly derives from his background. He was born at Lee's Summit, Missouri, "at a time when there was plenty of time," he says. "There wasn't a lot happening and you could make up your own stories and music. You couldn't follow what everybody else was doing because there weren't all that many people *to* follow. I used to sit playing the guitar and looking at the sky and wondering about the world beyond." It is hardly surprising that, to this day, there is the distinct air of a jazz Huckleberry Finn about Pat Metheny.

Metheny was something of a child prodigy. Although he only took up the guitar at age 13, he was teaching the instrument at the University of Miami before he was out of his teens. At 20 he joined Gary Burton's quartet and played on three of Burton's albums, leaving to form his own quartet with keyboard player Lyle Mays in 1977. Their basic style was a kind of smiling, melodic jazz-rock. The textures were light and the virtuosity understated, but the quartet could hold a packed festival audience enthralled.

Over the years, Metheny has experimented with many genres, even at one point touching on heavy metal, but he always comes back to this core idiom. "Let the notes ring," as he puts it. "Let the phrases sink in." On his 1979 album *New Chautauqua*, Metheny played the 12-string acoustic guitar, and in 1981 he featured a guitar synthesizer on *Offramp*, one of his most popular albums to date.

For an artist whose music has such strong atmospheric qualities, it is odd that Metheny has not created more film music than he has. His one major production in this field was the soundtrack to John Schlesinger's *The Falcon and the Snowman* in 1985. For this he collaborated with David Bowie, and one piece from the score, "This Is Not America," figured in the charts that year. Like much of his more recent work, the soundtrack reveals Metheny's masterly use of electronic shading. His touch is so delicate that the listener is hardly aware of the tonal depth that has been added to what is still essentially acoustic music. Perhaps the best example of this so far is *Beyond the Missouri Sky*, his 1997 collaboration with bassist Charlie Haden.

Pat Metheny remains one of the most personable and original artists in contemporary jazz. Thanks to his gift for melody and for creating attractive musical textures, he is also one of the most successful.

Like the music he creates, guitarist Pat Metheny retains the sparkle of youth and continues to attract young audiences. He has won numerous music industry awards, including a Grammy for the best contemporary jazz album of 1966 with *We Live Here*.

Charles Mingus

1 9 2 2 - 1 9 7 9

Charles Mingus's career as a jazz composer was blighted by anger and frustration. This was partly because of his own volatile and explosive personality, but mainly it was the result of an endless losing battle for the time and resources to bring his ambitious ideas to fruition. His intensity frightened people, including people who might have helped and supported him.

Although, by sheer willpower, he had made himself into a virtuoso of the double bass at the absurdly young age of 16, Mingus could never settle into the life of a jobbing musical craftsman. He began to experiment with composition in the early 1950s, and it soon became clear that he possessed an extraordinary talent. At a time when jazz musicians still tended to see themselves as part of the entertainment world, albeit a very special part, Mingus was producing pieces such as "Fables of Faubus," which mocked the notoriously racist Governor of Arkansas with derisive whoops and yells. This was typical Mingus, making a point of undercutting the listener's expectation by changing the mood, constantly shifting between seriousness and knockabout humor.

A bow-legged, shambling figure, Mingus exhorted his musicians through scores that they often complained were unplayable. And then, when some semblance of cohesion had been achieved, he would change his mind, tear the score to pieces, and start again. Yet he was also the master of the most delicate impressionism, a trait he shared with the one musician he admired totally, Duke Ellington. His 1957 album *Tijuana Moods* is a wonderfully sustained evocation of the life of a Mexican border town.

From a lifetime of lurid incident, the episode most often quoted took place on October 12, 1962. That evening, rushed and underprepared as usual, Mingus attempted to conduct a public recording session of some new music at New York Town Hall. Finding that the event had been billed as a normal concert, he first advised the audience to demand its money back, and then tried to achieve in three hours what Ellington would have done over several weeks of leisurely trial and error. Predictably, the result was a disaster.

Nobody knew at the time, but this was the first move in the creation of his biggest work, *Epitaph* ("because I'm writing it for my tombstone"). He continued working on it in secret, and it was not until after his death that his widow discovered the yellowing manuscript. *Epitaph* was performed triumphantly in 1991 by a 31-piece orchestra under the direction of musicologist Gunther Schuller.

If you look carefully, you will see that Mingus is drawing the bow underneath the strings instead of across the top—a technique that adds another unusual sound to his music.

Thelonious Monk

1917 - 1982

Thelonious Sphere Monk—what other name could match the man's music so perfectly? Unusual, even a little bizarre, but with an intriguing ring to it, Monk's music stands alone. He arrived on the scene with the bebop movement of the 1940s and, in a sense, he was the most complete bebopper of them all. He never made the slightest attempt to ingratiate himself with the public or even to acknowledge its presence, but created dauntingly spare and angular music by taking the harmonic innovations of Charlie Parker and Bud Powell and following them through with a kind of manic persistence.

Even insiders found Monk's music hard to take at the beginning, and throughout the 1940s and early 1950s, Monk worked little and recorded less. His music was self-defining, like a private language, and the only way into it was by listening and trying to follow. Typically, Monk offered no assistance. He refused to give press interviews or take part in any public activity other than the performance of music, and the only person in whom he would confide was his wife, Nellie. This was regarded as eccentric, but it was really only the self-defense of a stubbornly private man.

Monk's music changed very little in the course of his career. In fact, some of his very best recordings are the earliest, even though they were recorded under dreadful conditions in cheap studios. His most famous composition, "Round Midnight," has become a jazz standard over the years, but nothing surpasses his own first recording of it made in 1947—a somber, menacing mood piece, full of flitting shadows and midnight fears.

As a composer, Monk used the same methods as Jelly Roll Morton and Duke Ellington. He worked from inside the band, shaping and guiding the music, but actually writing very little. For this reason, he liked to work with the same musicians, such as saxophonist Charlie Rouse and trumpeter Ray Copeland, because they understood what he wanted without requiring endless explanations. This is how he created all his great recorded masterpieces: "Misterioso," "Criss Cross," "Little Rootie-Tootie," "Brilliant Corners," "Well, You Needn't," and more.

In the course of his life, Monk's public reputation passed through three distinct phases. At first he was seen as a harmless lunatic, then a fashionable eccentric, and finally, a revered elder statesman of jazz. It is entirely probable that Monk himself noticed none of this, except for the fact that he was working more regularly during the last two phases, and the pianos were more in tune.

Monk in 1950, wearing one of the more conservative items from his large collection of headgear, which included skullcap, fez, and Chinese field-worker's hat.

Wes Montgomery

1 9 2 3 - 1 9 6 8

After Charlie Christian, the next great innovator of the electric guitar was Wes Montgomery. To Charlie's long, single-note lines, Wes added solos in block chords and unison octaves, both still widely copied today. Apart from this, the most obvious difference between them is in the sound. Charlie plucked the guitar strings with a plectrum, while Wes used his thumb, producing a rounded warmth to the instrument's tone. If imitation is the sincerest form of flattery, then Charlie and Wes between them are the most flattered guitarists in jazz.

Strangely, for such an important and influential figure, Wes Montgomery came to prominence quite late in life. Born in Indianapolis, he took up the guitar as a teenager and was completely self-taught. With his two brothers, Monk and Buddy, on bass and vibraphone respectively, the trio was soon in great demand around the local clubs. Wes toured briefly with Lionel Hampton's band between 1948 and 1950, but returned home and settled back into the familiar routine. As a married man with a family, he held onto a daytime job until well into his thirties.

The brothers, calling themselves first the Mastersounds and later the Montgomery Brothers, recorded their first album in 1957. Wes continued to play and record with them, even when his own career took off spectacularly at the end of the decade. The album that finally did it was called *The Incredible Jazz Guitar of Wes Montgomery* (1960), his second release on Riverside, one of the top jazz labels of the time. There was scarcely a jazz fan in the world who did not at least hear it, and few serious students of jazz guitar who did not own a well-played copy of the album.

Montgomery was a modest and unassuming man, and his playing—for all its brilliance—was never flashy, a fact that probably contributed to his great popularity in later years. The music, like the man himself, was friendly and eminently approachable.

In 1964 Montgomery signed with Verve, a major international label. Under the guidance of producer Creed Taylor, he embarked on the series of albums that was to raise him out of the pure jazz category and into the wide, popular market previously conquered by artists such as Erroll Garner. His Verve albums brought him a huge worldwide audience, and while his original fans muttered that these were nowhere as good as the Riverside classics, they could not begrudge Wes his new-found star status. He died of a heart attack at the peak of his career.

Wes Montgomery toward the end of his life, when he had achieved great success with his hugely popular Verve albums, produced by Creed Taylor.

Jelly Roll Morton

1 8 9 0 - 1 9 4 1

The old show-business adage that you should be nice to people on your way up because you might meet them again on your way back down certainly applies to Ferdinand Joseph Lemott, otherwise known as Jelly Roll Morton. Bumptious, snobbish, and self-opinionated—not to mention suspicious, quarrelsome, and greedy—he managed to offend virtually everybody during his years of success. Later, when his luck ran out, no one raised a finger to help him. He even managed to upset the normally imperturbable Duke Ellington, who pointedly stayed away from his funeral.

But great artists do not have to be nice people, and Morton was a great artist. He may not have "invented" jazz, as he claimed, but he was a blindingly good pianist and the first major jazz composer. Born in New Orleans into a French-speaking Creole family, he was present during the melting-pot days, when jazz was just beginning to emerge. At a remarkably early age, he began playing the piano in brothels, for which he was effectively disowned by his respectable family. Setting out to make his fortune, he wandered the United States, ending up in Chicago in the early 1920s. On the way, he later claimed, he earned his living as a pianist, vaudeville comedian, pool shark, and pimp.

Morton's unchallenged status as an artist rests on two sets of recordings: the intricate and spirited piano solos from 1923 to 1924 and the almost miraculously perfect series made between 1926 and 1929 by his band, the Red Hot Peppers. These pieces amount to highly stylized versions of early New Orleans jazz, and they were produced by a method pioneered by Morton that might be termed "shaped improvisation." The musicians played in their usual styles and Morton snipped, tucked, and layered in rehearsal, inserting breaks and background figures, constantly varying the texture.

The effect is an effortless flow, so easy and natural that the sheer ingenuity with which Morton handled his seven instruments could easily escape notice. Peppers' numbers such as "Black Bottom Stomp," "The Chant," and "Grandpa's Spells" are among the timeless classics of jazz.

Morton was a great success in the 1920s. His band had the pick of society balls and rich people's parties. He owned a hundred suits and had a diamond set in his front teeth. But jazz grew and changed so quickly during his lifetime that he spent his last decade in oblivion, written off as corny and old-fashioned. He died just too soon to benefit from the New Orleans revival of the 1940s.

Jelly Roll Morton in later life. The records he made in his last years are filled with an aching nostalgia for the vanished New Orleans of his childhood.

Gerry Mulligan

1 9 2 7 - 1 9 9 6

Gerry Mulligan defined the voice of the baritone saxophone in modern jazz. Before he arrived on the scene in the late 1940s, the only baritone player of note had been Harry Carney of Duke Ellington's orchestra. Carney's massive tone and stately phrasing seemed to have defined the instrument's character for all time, but Mulligan's airy sound and agile phrasing expanded its expressive horizons immensely. At the same time, Mulligan was an important composer and arranger. The clear, sharply defined lines of his orchestration, along with the work of Gil Evans, John Lewis, and Miles Davis, led to a radically new style of writing when they collaborated on Miles's Birth of the Cool band in 1949. Of the 12 numbers recorded by this band, Mulligan wrote five.

Fame suddenly descended on Mulligan in 1952 with the launch of his first quartet, co-starring trumpeter Chet Baker. The band's lineup of baritone saxophone, trumpet, bass, and drums caused a sensation at first, since it contained no piano or other chordal instrument to lay down the basic harmonies. Although the idea was revolutionary, the quartet's music was beguilingly easy on the ear—far more attractive to the casual listener than most other small-band instrumental jazz of the period.

A Californian jazz lover, Richard Bock, was so taken with the sound that he borrowed money to record it. The first 10-inch LP by the Gerry Mulligan Quartet, released in 1952, was a runaway success, far exceeding Bock's wildest hopes and laying the foundations for his Pacific Jazz label, which grew to become the biggest West Coast jazz label of the 1950s and 1960s. Cool and fluent, with witty arrangements and tuneful solos, the quartet's music remains some of the most charming in the history of jazz.

A whole series of similar quartets followed, each one containing distinguished soloists, such as valve-trombonist Bob Brookmeyer and trumpeter Art Farmer. Mulligan the writer came to the fore with the launch of his 13-piece Concert Jazz Band in 1960. The music he created for this ensemble features some of the richest and most adventurous orchestral color outside the work of Duke Ellington, but although Mulligan managed to keep Concert Jazz Band going, on and off, into the mid-1970s, its subtle approach was unfashionable at the time.

In later years, Mulligan concentrated mainly on playing, although he formed occasional temporary bands along the lines of the Concert Jazz Band. He guested regularly with Dave Brubeck and traveled the world as a star soloist.

Mulligan, still sporting his college-boy haircut, rehearsing with his sextet in the mid-1950s. The player in the foreground is the great tenor saxophonist Zoot Sims.

Fats Navarro

1 9 2 3 - 1 9 5 0

Perhaps even more than Dizzy Gillespie, Fats Navarro is the father of modern jazz trumpet. This is partly because his playing was the model on which Clifford Brown constructed his style, and Clifford himself was massively influential on later generations of trumpet players. These include such major figures as Freddie Hubbard, Lee Morgan, Blue Mitchell, and Roy Hargrove. But Navarro was too great an artist in his own right to be filed away as a worthy ancestor. He died at the age of 26, so his body of recorded work is not large, but it contains some stupendously impressive playing.

Fats joined Andy Kirk's Clouds of Joy band at the age of 20, and in the following year, replaced Dizzy Gillespie in Billy Eckstine's orchestra, the first out-and-out bebop big band. Recordings of this amazing 16-piece outfit sound pretty ferocious, even by today's standards—in particular, a radio session from early 1945 in which the 21-year-old Fats plays a blistering solo on "Airmail Special."

For most of his short professional life—which coincided with the peak of the bebop movement—Fats worked as a freelance in New York, recording with most of the leading bop figures. He had a particularly close working relationship with the composer and band leader Tadd Dameron and featured on many of Dameron's finest records, including "Lady Bird," "The Squirrel," and "Our Delight." Dameron led small bands in which the single trumpet player, as well as playing solos, had to lead the ensemble. Whenever Navarro is in this role, his bright, forceful tone adds an extra sparkle to the whole band's sound.

It is when one hears him alongside other trumpeters that Fats' total mastery reveals itself. For example, he recorded in 1946 with a pickup band called Kenny Clarke's 52nd Street Boys, in which he and Kenny Dorham were the trumpet soloists. On the blues number "Royal Roost," Dorham comes up with a good, clean, imaginative solo, only to be completely flattened by Fats, who follows him with a demonstration of technique, invention, and sheer power that would put anyone in the shade—Gillespie included.

Fats' greatest attribute as an improviser was the remarkable ability to think in long musical sentences and to link them together into even longer musical paragraphs. No other trumpet soloist could touch him in this respect—until Clifford Brown came along.

But all this was before heroin got to Fats, lowering his resistance to the tuberculosis that lay dormant and then killed him at the age of 26.

Herman Leonard's classic action shot of Fats Navarro, captured at New York's Royal Roost Club in 1948, the high-water mark of bebop's brief popularity.

King Oliver

1 8 8 5 - 1 9 3 8

Nowadays, King Oliver's name is more familiar than his music among jazz lovers. There are two reasons for this. First, Louis Armstrong never tired of talking about his early days and the role that Oliver played in launching his career. Second, Oliver's best music was recorded so long ago, using such primitive technology, that it actually takes an effort to listen to it.

Joe Oliver rose as a young man to become the top cornet player in New Orleans, which is how he received the title of "King." This was in the days of jazz prehistory, before World War I, when the music that became jazz was largely confined to the city—in particular Storyville, its red-light district. When the district was closed down in 1917, musicians were thrown out of work. Many left New Orleans and, like Oliver, ended up in Chicago, where jazz first took root and flourished in the 1920s.

King Oliver's Creole Jazz Band—with almost all New Orleans migrants in its lineup—was the first big-name jazz band in the city, attracting crowds to Lincoln Gardens, the dance hall where it played every night. Once established in Chicago, Oliver sent for Armstrong to join him in 1922, thereby handing the young man his first big break. Louis, who scarcely knew his own father, always referred to Oliver as "Papa Joe" and regarded him as something of a father-figure. Oliver's fondness for the young man was tempered by shrewdness. "As long as I got him with me," he said, "he won't be able to get ahead of me."

The Creole Jazz Band, with Oliver and Armstrong as twin lead cornets, was indeed a glorious band. Even the early acoustic recording manages to convey the sweeping, unhesitating confidence of the ensemble, the confident intricacy of the interweaving lines, and the perfectly coordinated duet breaks executed by Oliver and Armstrong together. Oliver's own specialty was his use of mutes to create crying, "blue" phrases, exemplified by his most famous recorded solo in "Dipper Mouth Blues" (1923). The Creole Jazz Band broke up in 1924, amid much bad feeling and accusations that Oliver had been cheating the musicians out of their hard-earned money.

Oliver formed a new band, the Dixie Syncopators, which did well for some years, but slowly Oliver's luck deserted him. He failed to take account of changing fashions in music and began having trouble with his teeth, thus impeding his playing technique. By the mid-1930s, his career was at an end. He died in Savannah, Georgia, working as a janitor in a pool hall.

King Oliver's Creole Jazz Band in the 1920s (left to right): Baby Dodds (drums), Honore Dutrey (trombone), King Oliver (cornet), Bill Johnson (banjo and double bass), Louis Armstrong (cornet), Johnny Dodds (clarinet), and Lil Hardin (piano).

The Original Dixieland Jazz Band

1 9 1 7 - 1 9 2 5

Arguments rage about the origins and early history of jazz, but it is reasonably safe to say that the Original Dixieland Jazz Band's (ODJB) recording of "Livery Stable Blues," made on February 26, 1917, marks the beginning of recorded jazz. This is a somewhat inconvenient fact because "Livery Stable Blues" is a work of no great merit but a raucous gallop, replete with animal noises and other comic effects. But that is how jazz was first presented to the general public, as a vaudeville curiosity.

Another inconvenient fact, for some theorists, is that the ODJB was an all-white band. The conventional view of jazz history holds that black musicians invented jazz and white musicians copied them. If this is true, the very existence of the ODJB means that the process must have started a very long way back in jazz prehistory. On the other hand, the five members of the ODJB were all natives of New Orleans, and there is plenty of evidence that jazz was bubbling up everywhere in that city at the beginning of the 20th century.

The real importance of the ODJB lies in its role in taking jazz beyond the confines of New Orleans: first to New York, Chicago, and the cities of the north and eventually across the Atlantic. It was during its sensational appearance at Resenweber's Restaurant in New York that it made that historic first record. It was soon followed by others, and within a year or two, there were ODJB records spinning on clockwork phonographs across the United States.

Young people adored the music; older people often detested it, seeing it as a symptom of the new godless, sensation-seeking, postwar world. Nick LaRocca, the band's cornet-playing leader, stoked the fires of controversy with statements such as, "I confess we're musical anarchists!" When they traveled to London in 1919 to appear in a show starring comedian George Robey, they lasted just one night. The outraged Robey sacked them, but they were hired immediately by a rival theater. They stayed in England for more than a year and were even summoned to Buckingham Palace to play for a slightly bemused King George V.

In time, fashion overtook the ODJB. Their crazy antics, banging tin cans and imitating farmyard animals, quickly wore out their novelty value, and the five boys from New Orleans simply could not compete with the sleek efficiency of professional band leaders such as Paul Whiteman. LaRocca fell ill in 1925, and despite several later attempts to revive it, that was the end of the ODJB.

The Original Dixieland Jazz Band (left to right): Eddie Edwards (trombone), Nick LaRocca (cornet), Tony Sbarbaro (drums), Henry Ragas (piano), and Larry Shields (clarinet). Although the ODJB was promoted as an outlandish novelty, a significant minority of young people understood that there was much more to jazz than the band's seemingly frivolous antics.

Kid Ory

1 8 8 6 - 1 9 7 3

False modesty was never Kid Ory's style. He claimed, for instance, that he bought a trombone on a Wednesday and was playing it for money at a dance on Saturday. He was certainly a naturally gifted musician, so it may be true. He was also a natural businessman, putting on little shows and picnics around his hometown, La Place, Louisiana, before the age of 10.

As his name suggests, Edward Ory was born into a French-Creole family. At 21 he left home, traveled the 30 miles (50 km) to New Orleans, and found work as a musician. Before long he was leading his own band, promoting dances at several venues, and becoming a local celebrity. Many future greats of jazz passed through Ory's band in the early years of the 20th century, including King Oliver and the teenaged Louis Armstrong. Eventually, his various ventures prospered so well that they began affecting rival businesses owned by members of the underworld. In 1919, after a visit from "the boys," he hurriedly shut up shop and moved to Los Angeles.

Once again, he quickly built a reputation as a band leader. In 1921, during his stay in California, Ory made the first-ever recordings by a black New Orleans band—four sides for the Sunshine label, including his specialty number, "Ory's Creole Trombone." Meanwhile, the cream of New Orleans jazz had moved to Chicago, and in 1925 Ory joined them, invited by his former employee, King Oliver. His timing was perfect. Players from New Orleans preferred to work with others from the city, and trombonists were in short supply.

In quick succession, Ory recorded with Louis Armstrong's Hot Five, Jelly Roll Morton's Red Hot Peppers, and King Oliver's Dixie Syncopators—three of the greatest bands in jazz history. He made a lot of money and looked after it, returning to California in 1930. When the Depression laid waste to the music business, he gave up playing and ran a chicken farm.

In 1942 Ory's old friend, clarinettist Barney Bigard, persuaded him that there was a renewed interest in original New Orleans jazz and encouraged him to return to music. The new Ory band was a success, greatly helped by being featured weekly in Orson Welles' radio show, *Mercury Wonder*. In 1946 Ory was reunited with Armstrong in the film *New Orleans* (released in 1947). For the rest of his life, Ory, now a revered figurehead of the revivalist movement, toured the world playing the music of his youth to adoring crowds.

During his 86 years, Kid Ory enjoyed two successful careers in music, retiring to a safer occupation as a farmer during the Depression of the 1930s. He was renowned as a careful man with a dollar. His motto was: "Never blow a note that you're not being paid for."

Charlie Parker

1 9 2 0 - 1 9 5 5

Once one's heard it, one would know it anywhere. The sound of Charlie Parker's alto saxophone is unmistakable, like the sound of Louis Armstrong's trumpet or John Coltrane's tenor. It is not a comfortable sound. The tone is brusque, with a curious, thick-tongued articulation, like a lisp. At first hearing, Parker can seem incomprehensible, his solos a wild, illogical jumble. That is certainly how it sounded to most people in the 1940s, when his early records began appearing.

Parker, universally known as "Bird," was certainly a musical revolutionary, but like his great predecessor, Louis Armstrong, he represents the end of a tradition as well as something new. Just as Armstrong worked within the bounds of his native New Orleans idiom until they could no longer contain him, so Parker, having learned his craft in the hard school of Kansas City jam sessions, never challenged the basic materials with which he worked. Throughout his career, he built his improvisations on the same patterns he had mastered as a teenager—the 12-bar blues and 32-bar American song. But he found far more complicated shapes in the old blues and ballads than his elders would have believed possible.

To listen to Bird playing a simple blues is to hear a musical mind working on several tasks at once, at impossible speed. First, there are the notes, then their rhythmic placement, and, finally, the shape of the whole solo. In the notes department he was supreme, suggesting an ever-changing series of harmonic possibilities. While doing this, he would deploy phrases and accents in such a way that one could be tricked into thinking he had missed a beat until, several bars later, he casually picked up the dropped stitch and the whole thing came into line again. The amazing thing is not only that he could bring off such feats of concentration at will, but that he could do it when stoned to the eyeballs on gin, heroin, and anything else that happened to be available.

A large part of Bird's recorded legacy consists of ragged chunks, recorded by fans on location or off the radio. This was the earliest example of systematic sound bootlegging, made possible first by primitive wire-recorders and after 1948 by the first generation of tape-recorders. Whenever a producer managed to get Parker into a studio, the session could be a testing experience for all concerned. "Each and every enterprise involving Charlie Parker was chaotic and fraught with a sense of impending disaster," recalled Ross Russell, his biographer and owner of Dial Records. But if Russell and others had not persevered, we should not now have the priceless music that Parker so casually dispensed.

This characteristic shot dates from 1948, when Parker was leading his famous quintet in the clubs along New York's 52nd Street. People who saw him in action report that his bow tie bobbed up and down on his Adam's apple when he played.

Oscar Peterson

b. 1925

The worst thing anyone has ever said about Oscar Peterson is that he is too good at his job. The argument goes like this: Peterson possesses a phenomenal piano technique, which enables him to play effortlessly whatever comes into his mind, but the very absence of struggle results in music that is glib, flashy, and shallow.

None of this is true, but it goes down well with the grumpier elements in the jazz community. He certainly makes it look easy, but one only has to pay attention for a few minutes to realize that there is plenty of drama going on beneath the urbane surface. Take, for instance, those immaculate, high-speed runs that go bubbling up and down the keyboard, seemingly for minutes on end. With a glib pianist, these would be just decoration. Peterson takes one on a whirlwind chromatic tour, delving into all kinds of harmonic nooks and crannies before landing at exactly the right moment.

His biographer, Gene Lees, points out that Peterson studied in Montreal as a teenager with Paul de Marky, who studied with Stefan Thoman, who in turn studied with Franz Liszt. With such a background and an inclination toward jazz, it is hardly surprising that he became what he is—a jazz concert pianist.

Above: Oscar Peterson (piano), Ray Brown (bass), and Herb Ellis (guitar) play in the Jazz at the Philharmonic in the early 1950s.

In the 1950s, Peterson led his first trio—deliberately modeled on the King Cole Trio—consisting of himself, Herb Ellis on guitar, and bassist Ray Brown. This prodigious team set out to wipe the floor with any opposition foolish enough to present itself. With awesome single-mindedness and unremitting practice over several years, they forged an ensemble that was, in Ray Brown's words, "damn near waterproof."

Lees' biography was subtitled "The Will to Swing," and Peterson's ability to create instant, driving, unstoppable swing is indeed prodigious. It is this element that makes his playing uniquely enthralling. It also makes him one of the best-ever accompanists in jazz. Listen, for instance, to the two *Ella & Louis* albums (1957). He does not sink anonymously into the background, but neither does he seek to upstage the principals.

Peterson is one of the best-known jazz musicians ever and his name alone is enough to draw capacity audiences around the world.

Left: Peterson the jazz concert pianist has pursued a thoroughly respectable and well-ordered career under the careful management of impresario and manager Norman Granz, who first brought him from Canada to the United States.

Michel Petrucciani

1 9 6 2 - 1 9 9 9

"It's what you have in your head, not your body," Michel Petrucciani used to say. "When you're short, people think you're a kid and treat you that way." Petrucciani was certainly short. He suffered from osteogenesis imperfecta, or brittle-bone disease, and stood barely three feet (0.9 m) tall, weighing only 50 pounds (23 kg) as an adult. Despite his physical difficulties, though, he was one of the outstanding jazz pianists of his generation.

Petrucciani had a phenomenal technique and a seemingly endless fund of inventive ideas. So masterly was his playing that audiences forgot about his disability within a few minutes. The willpower that enabled him to triumph over his circumstances also gave him the ability to concentrate on music to the exclusion of other distractions.

Born of French-Italian parents at Orange, near Avignon, France, he first heard jazz at the age of four when Duke Ellington's orchestra appeared on television. His father borrowed an old piano and the child immediately began to teach himself. By the age of 10, he was playing in public. At first he modeled himself on Bill Evans, and although his own style quickly developed, something of Evans' harmonic subtlety stayed with Petrucciani for the rest of his career.

In 1977 the great American trumpeter Clark Terry was touring in France and looking for a pianist. On being introduced to the 15-year-old Petrucciani, he could scarcely believe what he was seeing and hearing, but was soon convinced and hired him. The news spread, and the following year, Petrucciani was in Paris, at the heart of the European jazz scene.

In 1982, having been awarded the Prix Django Reinhardt and voted French Jazz Musician of the Year, he left for the United States. He joined saxophonist Charles Lloyd's band, creating the same kind of stir that Keith Jarrett had caused when making his debut with Lloyd. The emphasis was still on his remarkable technique and the sheer density of his playing. It was not until 1985, when he signed with Blue Note and recorded the album *Pianism*, that his style reached its full maturity. After this came a string of glorious releases, including *Power of Three* (1986), *Music* (1989), and *Playground* (1991).

Petrucciani achieved all this even though repeated bone fractures kept him away from public performance for long periods. His affliction weakened his whole constitution and he died of a chest infection at the age of 37.

This characteristic action shot vividly illustrates Michel Petrucciani's small stature. Clearly visible is the attachment that allowed him to operate the pedals of the piano. None of this, however, distracted listeners from the brilliance of his playing, and his physical difficulties soon faded into the background.

Bud Powell

1924 - 1966

Bud Powell was to the piano what Charlie Parker was to the alto saxophone or Dizzy Gillespie to the trumpet. His playing virtually defined how the instrument should be played in the bebop idiom. At its best, Powell's playing had a crystalline brilliance that no one has ever equaled, before or since. He produced an endless flow of ideas, constantly changing rhythmic and harmonic patterns at such velocity that the sheer impetus of it leaves one gasping. At slow tempos, he enveloped the melody in a dense tapestry of decoration, each little phrase minutely detailed and beautifully articulated.

All these qualities are amply displayed in a set of eight numbers he recorded in January 1947 for the Roost label. In pieces such as "Bud's Bubble," "Indiana," and "Everything Happens to Me," he shows himself to be Parker's equal. He also plays with incandescent brilliance on a famous live recording of Parker and Gillespie, made at Massey Hall, Toronto, in 1953.

Unhappily, Bud Powell also suffered from a number of afflictions that, as the years passed, increasingly interfered with his talent. His recurrent bouts of mental illness may have been set off by a beating at the hands of the New York Police Department in 1945. Whatever the case, he spent several periods in hospital and was given electric-shock treatment on more than one occasion, which seems only to have made matters worse. In addition, he was addicted to heroin. His recordings from the mid-1950s onward tend to be erratic, sometimes as good as ever and sometimes uncertain and disjointed. Powell was painfully aware of his own condition, and several of his compositions bear titles that refer to it, for instance "Hallucinations," "Un Poco Loco," and "The Glass Enclosure," which portrays his sense of isolation.

Toward the end of the 1950s, he moved to Paris in an effort to escape the pressures of life in New York. He was befriended there by Francis Paudras, a jazz-loving artist who undertook his rehabilitation. Paudras became Powell's closest companion, overseeing every aspect of his life and keeping undesirable company at bay. Eventually, in 1964, Powell's health and confidence had improved to a point where he felt able to fly to New York for a series of engagements. He failed to return to Paris, as arranged, went back to his old habits, and died in August 1966. The story of Francis Paudras and Bud Powell was told, semifictionalized, in the 1986 film *Round Midnight*. In the same year, Paudras published his own account of their relationship in a book, *La Danse des Infidèles*.

Bud Powell playing at New York's Open Door Club in September 1953, the year in which he made a number of superb recordings for the Blue Note label.

Django Reinhardt

Django Reinhardt, the first great European jazz musician, was born in Belgium into a close community of Gypsy entertainers. By the age of 11, he was playing guitar, banjo, and violin for traditional French accordionists. In 1928 the caravan in which he was living caught fire and Django's left hand was badly burned. Although doctors managed to save the hand, his third and fourth fingers were paralyzed. With immense determination, he worked out a whole new method of fingering the guitar using his remaining fingers, and within two years, he was playing professionally again.

Until that time, Django had played purely French and Gypsy music and knew almost nothing about jazz. However, his travels took him to Nice, where Emile Savitry, a rich patron of the arts, introduced him to records by Louis Armstrong and Duke Ellington. Django understood their music instantly. He joined the popular bands of Louis Vola and André Ekyan, and through them made contacts in the growing European jazz scene.

One night, Reinhardt and Vola's violinist, Stephane Grappelli, were jamming backstage. Soon they were joined by another guitarist and Vola himself on bass. The result was a unique sound, light and springy, and they began working to develop it. With Django's brother, Joseph, added as a third guitarist, they were booked to play a concert for the Hot Club de France and caused a sensation. Under the name Quintette du Hot Club de France, the band made its first records in 1934 and continued to record regularly over the next five years.

Meanwhile, Django was being hailed as a star on his own account. As his fame spread, the attitude of American musicians visiting Paris changed from curiosity to respect. He was soon sitting in on recording sessions with jazz greats such as Coleman Hawkins, Benny Carter, and Dicky Wells.

The Quintette were touring England when World War II was declared in September 1939. Grappelli decided to remain in London, but Django returned to Paris. He remained there throughout the German occupation and, despite the Nazi hostility toward Gypsies, continued to play in public. He was reunited with Grappelli after the war, but the old camaraderie was no longer there and they drifted apart. Later in life, Grappelli admitted that Django's wayward and disorganized approach to his profession had caused him much distress.

In his last years, Django took up the electric guitar and flirted with bebop, but he devoted more time to fishing and painting than to music.

This famous portrait from the late 1940s clearly shows how Django played the guitar with his damaged left hand. Only the index and middle fingers had complete mobility.

Buddy Rich

1917 - 1987

Incredible though it may seem, Buddy Rich actually began playing the drums at the age of 18 months. His parents were a vaudeville double act, Wilson and Rich, and they introduced the infant Buddy into the show under the name of "Baby Traps." By the age of 11, he was a seasoned professional.

Coming of age in the swing era, he became a sought-after big-band drummer, playing first with Bunny Berigan, then Harry James, Artie Shaw, and, finally, Tommy Dorsey. By now he was renowned as the most powerful and driving of big-band drummers, with a personality and ego to match. This brought him into direct confrontation with Dorsey's equally pushy and determined male singer, the young Frank Sinatra. Their fights soon entered the realms of show-business legend. In fact, Sinatra narrowly escaped death once when Rich tried to brain him with a heavy glass water jug. Much later, when they were both in their sixties and Rich had suffered a heart attack, Sinatra paid all his hospital bills.

Rich formed his own first big band in 1945—exactly the wrong moment— and lost all his money in the venture. In 1947 he joined the touring show Jazz at the Philharmonic, where he developed his phenomenally fast and impressive solo drum routines. Rich also revealed some talent as a vocalist, and for a while considered changing careers to become a singer and actor. Instead, however, he joined the new and surprisingly successful band formed by Harry James in 1961 and stayed with it for five years.

The experience persuaded him that he could make a success of his own big band after all, and he launched it in 1966. Excellent arrangers and a crop of good soloists helped it to get started, but the focus of the band was always on Rich's own drumming. True to his vaudeville upbringing, he was a born showman and he delivered a show—slamming around the kit, drumsticks a blur of ceaseless movement—for 10 minutes at a stretch.

As he grew older, Rich's style became increasingly manic. Many drummers, and a certain type of big-band buff, looked upon him almost as a god, but musicians who worked for him told tales of high-handed behavior that would have shamed a third-world dictator. A bootleg tape of Rich ranting, bullying, and boasting about his war service in the Marines, secretly recorded on the band bus, was eagerly copied and circulated around the jazz world.

Right to the end, he displayed prodigious willpower, shrugging off repeated heart attacks and barnstorming around the globe for nine months a year.

Buddy Rich with his big band. In later years, this consisted almost exclusively of young players, fresh out of college. The experience was professionally valuable for them, but often personally traumatic.

Max Roach

b . 1 9 2 4

Max Roach is the father of modern jazz drumming. Jo Jones and Kenny Clarke prepared the way by lightening the texture and creating a more fluid approach to the beat, but it was Roach who brought it all together into a fully developed style. From the age of 10, he played drums in a gospel band, and as a teenager, studied percussion, musical theory, and composition at the Manhattan School of Music. He made his recording debut in Coleman Hawkins's band in 1943 at the age of 19, and was a constant attendee at the jam sessions at Minton's Playhouse and Monroe's Uptown House, where early bebop was hatched.

Most important of all, he was the drummer on virtually all Charlie Parker's recordings between 1946 and 1948, the years of the classic Parker Quintet. He was the first drummer to understand Parker's music well enough to create exactly the right kind of rhythmic support. His period with Parker was followed by two years with Miles Davis, during which time he took part in the celebrated *Birth of the Cool* recordings.

In 1954 Roach teamed up with Clifford Brown to co-lead their own quintet, which lasted until Brown's death in an automobile accident in 1956. This band, which also included Sonny Rollins on tenor saxophone during its final year, is generally credited as the originator of the style known as "hard bop." Brown and Roach brought out the best in each other's playing, and, fortunately, the quintet made plenty of records—both live and in the studio—which prove the fact. These include the albums *In Concert* and *Brown–Roach Inc.* (both 1954), *Study in Brown* (1955), and *At Basin Street* (1956).

In the late 1950s, Roach began to take an active role in the Civil Rights Movement, giving musical expression to its aspirations in albums such as *Deeds Not Words* (1958), *We Insist! Freedom Now Suite* (1960), and *It's Time* (1962). At the same time, he looked beyond the conventional jazz quintet format, creating music that incorporated percussion ensembles, choirs, and strings. *Percussion Bitter Sweet* (1961) is a particularly powerful album from this period.

Roach was always open to new ideas, and during the 1970s, worked with many of the leading figures in free jazz, such as Abdullah Ibrahim, Anthony Braxton, Archie Shepp, and Cecil Taylor. In 1970 he formed the percussion band M' Boom Re: Percussion, the 10 members of which play more than 100 percussion instruments between them. The band plays specially composed music, much of it owing as much to the African drum tradition as it does to jazz.

Max Roach in 1950, at the age of 26. He was already acknowledged as the leading drummer in contemporary jazz. Soon to follow was the classic partnership with Clifford Brown.

Sonny Rollins

b. 1930

The jazz world is full of tenor saxophonists, and a lot of them sound very much the same, but nobody sounds like Sonny Rollins. In the 1950s, Rollins was one of the two young heavyweights, the other being John Coltrane. It was Coltrane, with his exploration of modes, extended forms, and free improvisation, who turned out to be the more influential.

There is something of Coltrane in most tenor players under the age of 40. Rollins, on the other hand, was content to stick with the blues and the 32-bar American song, but what he can do with this basic material is quite tremendous. No other living jazz musician even attempts to create improvisations on the scale that he sets as his norm, employing such a rigorously restricted form in which to operate. His mental agility is simply unbelievable. Neither can any other living player equal the gutsy, cavernous roar of his tone.

Theodore Rollins was the indulged youngest child of a middle-class family and claims that he wasted much of his childhood "playing baseball and going to the movies." It was the second of these activities that laid the foundations of his unique repertoire, a vast and unlikely assortment of ancient show tunes in which he rummages happily. "All those hours in neighborhood movie houses, hours listening to the radio. I love those old tunes."

Rollins grew up a member of the bebop generation, and played with Charlie Parker, Miles Davis, and Max Roach, and just about every major figure from the late 1940s to the 1960s. The album that finally established him as one of the truly great figures in jazz was *Saxophone Colossus* (1956), a quartet session in which not a single note, accent, or breath could be altered without damaging the perfection of the whole. One piece in particular, "Blue 7," was analyzed at length by musicologist Gunther Schuller, who pointed out the complexity of Rollins' handling of his material. After reading it, Rollins claims, he was unable to play for a week. He said, "It was like riding a bicycle; if you think about what you're doing, you fall off."

Between 1959 and 1961, Rollins retired from public performance in order to practice and work out new ideas. One of his chosen practice places was the walkway of New York's Williamsburg Bridge because he could not be overheard up there. His first album after returning was actually entitled *The Bridge* (1962), and it unveiled a new, even broader tone, one that Rollins has retained and developed ever since.

Sonny Rollins in his shaven-head period of the late 1960s, when he was touring widely in Europe and Asia. It was during this time that he composed and recorded in London the soundtrack music for the 1966 film *Alfie*.

Artie Shaw

b. 1910

At the height of his success, at the close of the 1930s, Artie Shaw was among the biggest names in show business. He was reputed to be earning $60,000—more than half a million in today's terms—each week. His 1938 record of "Begin the Beguine" was a number one hit. His band was voted top swing band in the polls, he was a film star, with pin-up good looks, and about to marry Lana Turner, one of the most beautiful women in the world. And then, in November 1939, he walked away from it all. The reason, as he later explained, was that he simply could not come to terms with the fairground aspect of the entertainment business. He found it boring and demeaning.

Shaw was by nature an intellectual, with wide interests in literature, classical music, and the world of ideas. He was also a superb clarinet player, with a dark, plangent tone and a phenomenally sharp technique. He was a man full of paradoxes. Alongside his fastidiousness there went the reputation for being a Hollywood Romeo. Among his eight wives were film stars Lana Turner, Ava Gardner, and Evelyn Keyes; Kathleen Windsor, author of the bestseller *Forever Amber*; and Betty Kern, daughter of the songwriter Jerome Kern.

Shaw was to walk away and return several more times before finally giving up music in 1954. He returned in 1940, with another hit record, "Frenesi," and launched a superb small band, the Gramercy Five. When the United States entered World War II in 1941, Shaw folded his band and volunteered for the U.S. Navy in 1942. He led a band for 18 months in the South Pacific, while almost constantly under fire.

When they returned home, Shaw and his men were given immediate medical discharges. Once he had recovered, he set about forming another band, which included a new version of the Gramercy Five. This lasted until 1947, when Shaw decided to devote himself to classical music.

For two years he studied and appeared as a clarinet soloist with symphony orchestras, before setting up another band. But he had become bored with big bands. He retired to write his autobiography, *The Trouble with Cinderella*, which was published in 1952 to excellent reviews.

His last couple of years in music were spent leading a new Gramercy Five. He was playing better than ever—so well, in fact, that he decided he would never be able to improve on the standard he had reached. He again announced his retirement, and this time he stuck to it.

Artie Shaw around the time when his "Begin the Beguine" was top of the hit parade. A man of enormous energy and wide interests, he outlived all his famous contemporaries.

George Shearing

b. 1919

George Shearing was born blind, the result he suspected of an attempted abortion. As the child of a London coal man, he had no advantages in life, save for the gift of perfect pitch. He began picking out tunes on the piano at the age of three, and was taught the instrument formally at a school for the blind. By the age of 16, he was able to imitate the styles of most leading jazz pianists with uncanny accuracy and was hailed as a prodigy by the British jazz world. Readers of Britain's leading music paper, *Melody Maker*, voted him the nation's top jazz pianist for seven years in succession.

In 1947 Shearing emigrated to the United States and soon found work in the flourishing clubs along 52nd Street. This was the height of the bebop period, and Shearing concentrated on assimilating the music of Bud Powell and other masters of the style. He formed his own quintet, with a lineup of vibraphone, guitar, piano, bass, and drums, and devised a unique and distinctive sound for it. The melody was played by vibraphone and guitar in octaves, paralleled by tightly voiced piano chords. The effect was light and tuneful, and attractive to people who would not normally be attracted to jazz at all.

In 1949, with the release of the quintet's record of "September in the Rain," which sold 900,000 copies in the United States alone, Shearing found himself a popular star. Even at its most popular, however, the quintet still remained a jazz ensemble, and Shearing's own imaginative solos retained many traces of Bud Powell's influence. Among the George Shearing Quintet's biggest hits were "I'll Remember April" in 1950, "Pick Yourself Up," also in 1950, and Shearing's own composition "Lullaby of Birdland" in 1952.

So distinctive was the quintet's sound that it was borrowed wholesale. Arrangers incorporated "Shearing" passages into big-band scores, and every nightclub scene in every movie was accompanied by an imitation Shearing Quintet on the soundtrack. This went on well into the 1960s, long after Shearing himself had moved on to other things. He turned for a while to Latin music, scoring another hit with "Mambo Inn" in 1954.

Shearing's career has been dotted with superb collaborations with singers, from the classic *Beauty and the Beat* with Peggy Lee (1959), to a long and fruitful partnership in the 1980s and 1990s with Mel Tormé. His artistry seemed to expand as his years advanced, and Shearing at 80 was playing with the fire and imagination of a man half his age.

The young George Shearing in 1950, at the peak of his success with the quintet and its charming, lightweight adaptation of bebop. Shearing was the first British musician to become a leading figure on the U.S. jazz scene.

Horace Silver

b. 1928

Horace Silver's simple, feel-good tunes and joyful piano have been a valued part of jazz since the 1950s. Whole generations of young musicians have grown up learning to play numbers such as "The Preacher," "Sister Sadie," "Doodlin," and "Nica's Dream"—all Silver compositions—as part of their education.

His quintet, originally formed as a splinter group from Art Blakey's first Jazz Messengers in 1956, virtually defined the term "hard bop." He has rarely departed from the classic hard bop lineup of trumpet and tenor saxophone with rhythm section. No one has ever surpassed the ingenuity with which he uses these limited resources, juxtaposing unison and harmony, bringing in backing figures and bridge passages at just the right moment, but never interrupting the flow by over-arranging.

Although born in Connecticut, Silver is of Portuguese descent (his family name is actually Silva), and some of his compositions bear traces of the folk music of his father's native Cape Verde Islands.

He was leading the house trio at a club in Hartford, Connecticut, when Stan Getz appeared there as a guest soloist. Getz was so impressed by the trio's work that he hired them all on the spot to work as his touring band. It was Getz who first recorded three of Silver's compositions in 1950.

After freelancing for a while in New York, Silver was signed by Blue Note Records in 1952 and remained as a mainstay of the label for the next 28 years. Throughout the 1950s and 1960s, the appearance of each new Horace Silver album brought a fresh supply of future jazz standards—"Song for My Father," "Blowin' the Blues Away," "Señor Blues," and many more.

His own piano style is unmistakable. At first, it sounds too forceful to make a good accompaniment, but, as Stan Getz discovered long ago, this is not so. Silver propels the soloist's line without overwhelming it. His own solos usually follow a pattern of gradually increasing tension—long, rolling phrases, liberally sprinkled with quotations from a variety of unlikely sources. He is a hugely energetic player and ends each live set looking absolutely exhausted, but happy.

In later years, Silver has experimented with larger groups of brass, strings, and even choirs—including *Silver 'n' Brass* (1975), *Silver 'n' Voices* (1976), and *Silver 'n' Strings Play the Music of the Spheres* (1978)—in conjunction with the standard quintet. Between 1970 and 1972, he composed both music and lyrics for a three-album work, *The United States of Mind*.

Horace Silver in 1956, at the beginning of his band-leading career. He habitually plays hunched over the keyboard in this way. At the end of a long solo, his nose practically touches the keyboard.

Art Tatum

1 9 0 9 - 1 9 5 6

In the 1940s, when there was virtually no contact between jazz and classical music, distinguished figures of the classical world, such as Vladimir Horowitz, Walter Giesking, and Arturo Toscanini, could occasionally be spotted in basement clubs along 52nd Street. They had come to marvel at a half-blind piano-playing wonder named Art Tatum, whose technique and general musical brilliance seemed to them almost superhuman. It still does.

Tatum was unique. Starting with the basic "stride" piano style, perfected by Fats Waller, he added layer upon layer of elaboration, complex runs, and arpeggios, until the original tune was submerged in a sea of glittering notes. This was not simply a matter of fancy decoration, either. The runs would suddenly change direction, cutting across the beat and altering the shape of the whole piece. To complicate matters further, Tatum would change key without warning, continue in the new key until the listener's ear had adjusted, and then change back again.

These practices made him a great favorite with the younger generation of players, as well as with those of his own vintage. Fats Waller, on being told that Tatum had just walked into the club where he was playing, once announced, "Ladies and gentlemen, God is in the house tonight!"

Not surprisingly, Tatum worked mainly as a soloist or with his own trio of piano, bass, and guitar. When teamed with other players, he often crowded them out, not intentionally but because his imagination simply ran away with him. Everyone was so in awe of him that few protested, although Ben Webster once stopped playing, leaned across the piano, and remonstrated: "Art, do you mind? You've played your solo, now let me play mine!"

Tatum possessed an enormous repertoire and made literally hundreds of records during his career. In December 1953 the jazz impresario Norman Granz made a gallant attempt to capture the vast riches of Tatum's talent and experience by setting up an open-ended session and inviting him to play whatever he liked, for as long as he liked. Tatum played for two nights and a day, with brief intervals for sleep and refreshment, and there was still much more that he wanted to record. Further sessions were held in April 1954 and January 1955, and the results were eventually released on 12 albums, entitled *The Tatum Solo Masterpieces* (1975). For once the overused term "masterpiece" was fully justified.

Pianists still revere Art Tatum. Many have been influenced by him, but none has ever been so unwise as to try copying him.

Art Tatum listening to a playback during his marathon series of solo recordings in the mid-1950s, released later as *The Tatum Solo Masterpieces.*

Cecil Taylor

b. 1929

"In white music the most admired touch among pianists is light. The same is true among white percussionists. We in black music think of the piano as a percussive instrument. We beat the keyboard, we get inside the instrument." This statement by Cecil Taylor may act as a way into his music, which many listeners find difficult to the point of impossibility.

It is probably not very helpful to think of Taylor's music as jazz, but more as part of a new world of improvised music that has its roots in jazz but has developed a separate tradition and its own aesthetic over the past 40 years. Taylor certainly began his career in the conventional jazz way, playing piano in the bands of Johnny Hodges, Hot Lips Page, and Lawrence Brown. By the end of the 1950s, however, he had adopted a more abstract approach. This was a time when inquisitive artists of all kinds were seeking new modes of expression, and jazz was no exception.

The jazz innovator to make the biggest impact was Ornette Coleman, and so much attention was concentrated on him that others, including Taylor, tended to be overlooked. Despite the support of Gil Evans, who devoted one side of his 1961 album *Into the Hot* to his music, Taylor was virtually ignored for several years, and had to take menial jobs in order to survive. In 1966, however, he recorded two albums for Blue Note, *Unit Structures* and *Conquistador!*, which laid the foundations of a considerable reputation.

The new, abstract music dispensed with the regular beat of jazz and also with tonality—the conventional notion of key. This presented challenges that relatively few listeners were prepared to take up. But "free" music was not only free of musical convention, it was free of culturally specific features, too. This meant that it could find audiences as readily in Europe or Japan as in America.

Beginning with a European tour in 1969, Taylor's career has been pursued almost as much overseas as at home. Taylor, whose mother was a dancer, has taken a particular interest in creating music for dance. In 1979 he composed a ballet, *Tetra Stomp*. "I try to imitate on the piano the leaps in space that a dancer makes," he once said.

As a young man, Taylor studied both at the New York College of Music and the New England Conservatory, and he has had a parallel career as an academic in later years, teaching at a succession of colleges. He was awarded a Guggenheim Fellowship in 1973.

Cecil Taylor's keyboard technique is highly unorthodox and uses a great deal of physical energy. This reflects his view that the piano is a percussive instrument.

JACK TEAGARDEN
In Paramount Pictures

Jack Teagarden

1905 - 1964

Born only four years after Louis Armstrong, Teagarden was one of the pioneers of jazz. His lyrical, easy-swinging style finally rescued the trombone from the raucous, foot-in-the-slide comedy role to which it had previously been consigned and gave it dignity. He also sang, in a soft, warm, blurry voice that expressed his personality to perfection.

Jack Teagarden was said to be the first white jazz musician to play and sing the blues with natural assurance. He came from a part of Texas where the races lived together in rare harmony, and as a child he loved listening to the music of itinerant bands, gospel groups, and traveling tent shows of all kinds. The blues was part of his native language. A member of a large musical family, he took up the trombone as a child, when his arms were still too short to reach all seven positions of the slide. He worked out a way to play using only the first three positions and never bothered to change, causing trombonists ever afterward to wonder how he managed it.

Teagarden arrived in New York at age 22, already an experienced musician, and was instantly hailed as one of the leading players. There was a lot of recording going on at the time, much of it requiring adaptable musicians who could throw together an ad hoc arrangement and play the occasional hot chorus. Teagarden was in his element, and much in demand. A typical recording band of the period was the Venuti–Lang All-Stars, led by violinist Joe Venuti and guitarist Eddie Lang, with Jack, his trumpet-playing brother Charlie Teagarden, and the young Benny Goodman on clarinet. The casual elegance of these 1931 sessions has rarely been surpassed.

Teagarden formed his own big band in 1939. A man less cut out to be a band leader it would be hard to imagine. Apart from being the original Mr. Nice Guy and the world's softest touch, Jack was a drinker on the grand scale. Furthermore, this was wartime, and simply transporting a band around the country was a task of epic proportions. In 1947, having lost all his savings, Teagarden finally gave in and teamed up with Louis Armstrong to form the All-Stars. The close and unaffected friendship between the two was symbolized by their famous vocal duet number "Rockin' Chair."

Afterward, Teagarden toured and recorded as a soloist or with all-star pickup bands. One of his last albums, *Think Well of Me* (1962), is the musical equivalent of a warm, glowing sunset, the mellowest sound in the world.

In this publicity photograph from the late 1930s, Jack Teagarden is pushing the trombone slide to its fullest extent, something he never did when actually playing.

McCoy Tyner

b. 1938

It is impossible to imagine how jazz would have developed without the John Coltrane Quartet of the early 1960s, and difficult to see how Coltrane himself would have brought about his great innovations without the presence of McCoy Tyner as the quartet's pianist. Tyner evolved a whole new approach to harmony and the role of the piano in the rhythm section. His unique way of voicing chords to create great washes of harmonic color exactly matched the rolling, driving style of Elvin Jones, the quartet's drummer. It was on this foundation that Coltrane built his finest work.

Tyner began playing piano as a child in Philadelphia and was leading his own little band at the age of 15. At 21 he was a member of the Jazztet, a fine and sadly undervalued band co-led by Art Farmer and Benny Golson, and joined Coltrane the following year. It was the originality of the youthful pianist's style that appealed to Coltrane. "He gets a very personal sound from his instrument," he noted in an interview. "In addition, McCoy has an exceptionally well-developed sense of form." It was this sense of form that enabled him to give shape and drama to the very long improvisations that were a particular feature of the John Coltrane Quartet's work.

After leaving Coltrane in 1965, Tyner formed his own trio and continued to develop his unique style. He signed with Blue Note Records, and his first album under the new contract, *The Real McCoy* (1967), with tenor saxophonist Joe Henderson, is still regarded as one of the finest small-band records of the decade.

During the general slump in the jazz business of the late 1960s and early 1970s, Tyner worked briefly in such unlikely contexts as the Ike and Tina Turner Revue, but his artistic reputation continued to grow. With the issue of his albums *Sahara* (1972) and *Enlightenment* (1974), it was clear that he had built on his formative period with Coltrane and grown into one of the most important figures in contemporary jazz.

McCoy Tyner's career has benefited greatly from the internationalization of jazz over the past 25 years. His audience is worldwide, and his music is as appreciated and well understood in Europe and Asia as it is in the United States. This, in turn, has broadened his own musical horizons, prompting him to listen to the music of many cultures and allowing it to flow into his own material. These influences can be heard subtly at work in later recordings such as *The Turning Point* (1992) and *Infinity* (1995).

McCoy Tyner in the 1990s. Although his style has broadened over the years, it still has the distinctive open harmonies and lyrical phrasing of his Coltrane period.

Sarah Vaughan

1924 - 1990

Billie Holiday and Ella Fitzgerald were children of the swing era. The third great female jazz singer of the 20th century was Sarah Vaughan, and she was a child of bebop. Extravagantly gifted, with an ear of fearsome accuracy, an unshakable sense of time, and a voice of operatic range, she fully qualified for the over-worked title of "diva."

Sarah entered the music business at the age of 19, as relief pianist with Earl Hines' orchestra. When vocalist and occasional trumpeter Billy Eckstine left Hines the following year, 1944, to form his own band, Sarah left with him to be the new band's female singer. Eckstine's was the first bebop big band, and Sarah soon proved to be perhaps the only vocalist at the time capable of hand-ling the very "unvocal" intervals, and of pitching notes accurately against the unfamiliar harmonies of bop.

It was fitting that her first post-Eckstine recording should be with Charlie Parker and Dizzy Gillespie, in 1945. That single number, "Lover Man," laid the foun-dations of her solo career. One quality shines through all Sarah's records from the 1940s and 1950s, and that is a sensuous delight in the actual act of singing. One can hear her simply reveling in her own dexterity as she soars effortlessly through a barrage of flattened fifths, augmented ninths, and other harmonic bear-traps that

Above: Sarah at the second JVC Jazz Festival, Newport, in August 1985.

would defeat most other singers. There is a delicious moment in her 1953 version of "Just Friends," a ballad performance with strings in which she is clearly on her best behavior and singing absolutely straight. After the instrumental interlude, she comes back with a little pirouette, followed by a death-defying swoop that says, "See what I could do with this tune if I wanted to?"

Most singers' voices drop in pitch as they get older, but Sarah outdid every-one in this respect. During her last two decades, she could descend quite com-fortably into the baritone range, while still being able to reach her younger contralto. During those years, too, she at last achieved the status of a concert artist and no longer had to pay lip service to pop fashion. Essentially, she was an in-person performer, and some of her best albums are live recordings.

Left: Sarah in 1949, the year she signed with Columbia—her first contract with a major record label and the start of a tense relationship with the popular music industry.

Fats Waller

1 9 0 4 - 1 9 4 3

Thomas "Fats" Waller was the greatest of all stride pianists. ("Stride" refers to the player's left hand, marching purposefully along, marking time.) His influence in this capacity was enormous, and his disciples included Art Tatum, Teddy Wilson, Count Basie, and even Thelonious Monk. But the world at large came to know him as an inspired entertainer and the composer of such timeless popular songs as "Honeysuckle Rose" and "Ain't Misbehavin'."

It was not until the final decade of his life that Fats, the larger-than-life character, the derby-hatted mountain of jollity, became a public personality. From his late teens, he had been revered among musicians for his piano playing, his songs, and the pieces he composed for the piano, such as "Alligator Crawl" and "Clothes Line Ballet." He was also famed for the legendary quantities of gin he could consume without apparent ill effect. Then, in 1934, he was playing, singing, and generally clowning around at a party given by George Gershwin, when another guest, a recording executive, invited Fats to repeat the performance in the studio. They put together a small band, called it Fats Waller and his Rhythm, and left him to get on with it.

In just over nine years, Fats and his Rhythm recorded around 450 three-minute numbers for RCA Victor, sometimes up to 10 tunes per session, and a vast number of them were international hits—"Your Feet's Too Big," "I'm Gonna Sit Right Down and Write Myself a Letter," "The Joint Is Jumpin'," "My Very Good Friend the Milkman," and literally dozens more. The material varied from excellent to dire, but Fats didn't seem to mind. If the song was not much good, he would send it up unmercifully by peppering the performance with silly remarks or lapsing into gargling parody. But no matter how disrespectful the treatment, the music always swung impeccably. Fats's piano chorus was always a model of invention and rhythmic flow.

At the time of his death, Fats was still on his way up. His brief appearance in the 1943 film *Stormy Weather*, starring Lena Horne, almost stole the show, and it seemed that he was set to rival Louis Armstrong in the public's affections. But Fats, never one to look after himself, continued to eat, drink, smoke, and carouse at all hours. In addition, this was wartime, and Fats filled every spare moment by giving free shows for the armed forces. At age 39 he died suddenly, of pneumonia, on a train approaching Kansas City in a howling blizzard.

Fats performing "Ain't Misbehavin'" in the nightclub scene from *Stormy Weather*. Like most entertainers, he created an instantly recognizable public persona. The derby hat, shirt sleeves, mischievous grin, rolling eyes, cigarette, and handy gin bottle were all part of it.

Ben Webster

1 9 0 9 - 1 9 7 3

The sound of Ben Webster's tenor saxophone is one of the glories of jazz. It has a depth and luminosity that draws us in and involves us inextricably in what he has to say. The authority of it can stop conversations and could, in person, reduce a brawling mob of nightclub patrons to utter silence and stillness. It was his time with Duke Ellington's band from 1940 to 1943 that established Webster as a major figure. His solos on such pieces as "Cotton Tail," "All Too Soon," and "Just A'Sittin' and A'Rockin'" are timeless classics.

Former Ellington musicians often had difficulty in establishing themselves away from the charmed circle of his orchestra, but Ben Webster proved the exception. He thrived throughout the 1950s, traveling as a soloist with Jazz at the Philharmonic and recording regularly with everyone from Coleman Hawkins to Fred Astaire. For some years he lived in Los Angeles, providing a home for his mother and a number of ancient aunts while taking advantage of the buoyant Hollywood studio scene.

In the 1960s, the jazz climate changed radically, and players of Webster's generation began to find work opportunities drying up. With the death of his mother in 1964, he moved to Europe, settling first in Holland, where he lodged with an elderly lady who bossed him around just as his mother had done. He later moved to Copenhagen, where he worked regularly at the Montmartre Club and guested with the Danish Radio Orchestra. A recording from 1970 of Ben rehearsing the orchestra is wonderfully revealing about his meticulous approach to performance. At the time of his death, he was in the process of taking Danish citizenship. His estate is administered by the Danish Crown.

Ben Webster was a very strange man. Most of the time he was the most amiable of characters, but beyond a certain alcoholic threshold he became a raging beast, completely out of control, before passing out. He was also prone to doing bizarre things on sudden impulse. Once, finding himself in an elevator with Joe Louis, he punched the former world heavyweight champion in the stomach without warning. Louis, with his boxer's reflexes still in full working order, punched him back, knocking him out cold.

Despite these idiosyncrasies, Webster was a great artist, a romantic poet of jazz, and a true original. The beauty of his tone matched the melting elegance of his phrases to form a unique, instantly recognizable saxophone style that was as personal as a fingerprint.

Ben Webster at Birdland, New York, in 1949. His hooded eyes gave him a permanently mournful expression, but he was actually pleasant and amusing company—except when drunk.

Tony Williams

1 9 4 5 - 1 9 9 7

When the young drummer Anthony Williams made his debut with Miles Davis at the age of 17, listeners simply could not believe what they were hearing. Apart from his complete technical mastery, his playing revealed an utterly original rhythmic approach. With his arrival, the business of laying down a beat acquired complexities undreamed of by earlier generations of drummers. The whole thing can be heard happening on the live album *Miles Davis in Europe* (1963).

Herbie Hancock joined Miles Davis at around the same time, and with Ron Carter on bass, they grew into one of the finest rhythm sections jazz has ever known. They could retain the pulse of the music while suspending and stretching the beat almost to breaking point, implying rhythms that were not actually being played. It required concentration to follow them, and the passage of time has not made their feats sound any less miraculous. When Wayne Shorter joined the band in 1964, the classic Miles Davis Quintet of the 1960s was complete. At the same time, Williams was recording on his own account for the Blue Note label. In two excellent albums, *Lifetime* (1964) and *Spring* (1965), he created abstract, free-form jazz that owed nothing to the dominant Ornette Coleman school, and was much concerned with tone and texture.

Williams left Miles Davis in 1969 to create a jazz-rock "supergroup," also known as Lifetime, with guitarist John McLaughlin and organist Larry Young (bass guitarist Jack Bruce joined briefly later). They met with reasonable success, but made nothing like the splash they had intended. The problem with Lifetime was that there was simply too much going on for the listener to be able to grasp the thread of the music. The band broke up in 1973.

Throughout the later 1970s, Williams, Hancock, and Carter frequently reunited to form VSOP, a quintet playing in the style they had pioneered with Miles Davis. It was hugely popular and as accomplished as ever, although it inevitably suffered from the absence of Miles himself. It seemed as though Williams had no challenges left and no focus for his brilliance. He played as a guest with all the leading figures, including Sonny Rollins and Wynton Marsalis, but his career seemed to have grown shapeless.

Then, in the late 1980s, he teamed up with trumpeter Wallace Roney and found his form again, particularly on two albums, *Native Heart* (1989) and *The Story of Neptune* (1991), where he plays with all the fire and intricacy of his youth. He died at 51 of a heart attack following an operation.

Tony Williams playing with VSOP in the late 1970s. The apparent ease with which he could bring off impossible rhythmic feats was the despair of other drummers.

Lester Young

1 9 0 9 - 1 9 5 9

In the early 1930s, there was only one way to play the tenor saxophone in jazz, and that was Coleman Hawkins' way—big-toned, forceful, unyielding. And then along came Lester Young with his quite different approach—light, glancing, airy—which completely upset the scheme of things. From the day in 1936 when Lester first entered a recording studio, the tenor saxophone acquired two contrasting voices, and this duality has continued down to the present.

Lester was 27 years old, quite an advanced age for a debut, when he recorded that first session with a small group from Count Basie's band. There were some at the time who refused to take him seriously because he sounded so different, but within a couple of years, when Basie's band had become established, Lester Young was a jazz star.

There is no more perfect or consistent body of recorded work in jazz than the music he created between 1936 and 1941 with Basie, with Billie Holiday, and with various small bands such as the Kansas City Seven. The recordings with the young Billie Holiday, in particular, are among the great masterpieces of jazz—numbers such as "Me, Myself and I," "Foolin' Myself," and "Back in Your Own Backyard." It was Billie who named him "Pres"—short for "The President"—and he named her "Lady Day."

At the end of 1940, Lester left Basie and had a brief shot at leading his own band, but he did not have the temperament for it. After freelancing for a while and playing in his brother Lee's band, he rejoined Basie in 1943. In the same year, he appeared in a short film, *Jammin' the Blues*, which was nominated for an Academy Award. But immediately filming was over, the U.S. Army caught up with him and he was drafted. Marijuana and other substances were found on him and he was sentenced to 18 months' military detention. With remission, he was out in a year, but he bore the mental scars for the rest of his life.

Lester's postwar career was an up-and-down affair. He toured with Jazz at the Philharmonic, led his own small band, and recorded prolifically. Much of his recorded output, especially from the early 1950s, is magnificent. Gradually, however, his health declined and he found it increasingly difficult to play. Younger players, his own devoted followers, were doing better than he was, and the knowledge depressed him. He was taken ill while appearing in Paris, flew home to New York, and died at the age of 49. He had predicted that he would not live to see his 50th birthday.

This famous shot from the late 1930s shows Lester's extraordinary way of holding the tenor saxophone when he was a young man. As the years passed, the instrument gradually assumed its normal position.

Index